# Coping with Life's Traumas

# Coping with Life's Traumas

## Gladeana McMahon

Newleaf

Newleaf
an imprint of
Gill & Macmillan Ltd
Hume Avenue, Park West, Dublin 12
with associated companies throughout the world
www.gillmacmillan.ie
© Gladeana McMahon 2000
0 7171 2895 4
Design by Vermillion
Print origination by Carole Lynch
Printed by ColourBooks Ltd, Dublin

This book is typeset in Sabon 10.5pt on 16pt

All rights reserved. No part of this publication may be copied, reproduced or transmitted in any form or by any means, without permission of the publishers.

A CIP catalogue record for this book is available from the British Library.

1 3 5 4 2

# Contents

1. Understanding Trauma and Stress — 1
2. What is Post-Traumatic Stress Disorder (PTSD)? — 11
3. Common Post-Traumatic Stress Symptoms: Coping with Flashbacks, Intrusive Thoughts/Images and Sleep Difficulties — 19
4. The Ripple Effect and Secondary Traumatising by the Media — 35
5. Childbirth and Losing a Child — 44
6. Our Assumptions About the World: How Thinking Style Helps or Hinders — 59
7. Bereavement, Divorce and Relationship Break-Up — 86
8. Job Loss — 103
9. Sexual Assault and Domestic Violence — 112
10. The Cost of Caring — Prolonged Duress Stress Disorder (PDSD) — 124
11. Cults — 132
12. Critical Incident Stress Debriefing and Emergency Services Personnel and Trauma — 137
13. How to Choose a Therapist — 149
14. New Treatments — 158
15. More Ways to Help Yourself: Overcoming Depression, Guilt, Anger and Anxiety — 162
16. Life After Trauma — 192

Useful Addresses — 194

Further Reading — 206

CHAPTER 1

# Understanding Trauma and Stress

The 1995 edition of the *Oxford English Dictionary* describes trauma as an emotional shock following a stressful event, sometimes leading to long-term neurosis. The words trauma, traumatic and traumatised are now commonly used in everyday conversations. For the ordinary person, it means an event which is extremely unpleasant, personally shocking and which causes distress.

For those in the helping professions, the term trauma is usually applied to certain particular types of experiences. Health professionals will be looking for a range of signs and symptoms normally associated with experiencing a traumatic event. The criteria for Post-Trauma Stress and Post-Traumatic Stress Disorder are set out in the *Diagnostic Statistical Manual of Mental Disorders of the American Psychiatric Association* (DSM IV is the abbreviation used for the fourth edition), a key reference book used by doctors all over the world. Counsellors, psychologists and psychotherapists also use the same criteria to determine the type of psychological problems experienced by the person seeking help from them.

Post-trauma stress relates to a range of physical, emotional, psychological and behavioural signs and symptoms which a person may experience following a traumatic incident. If the incident contained elements of threats to personal safety or the safety of loved ones, or was overwhelming in intensity (with the person feeling extreme fear or helplessness), the counsellor may begin to consider the possibility of Post-Traumatic Stress Disorder (PTSD).

However, there are many types of life events which do not meet the criteria laid down in *DSM IV* for diagnosing Post-Traumatic Stress Disorder, but which can leave an individual severely damaged nonetheless. Using the words of Dr Rachel Yehuda, a USA-based practitioner and researcher into the area of PTSD speaking at a UK Conference for health care professionals, 'Our biology does not read textbooks. It simply reacts to a situation.' Someone with a severe grief reaction could still experience the signs and symptoms associated with PTSD even though, according to the current diagnostic criteria, the incident itself did not qualify as traumatic.

The criteria for diagnosing Post-Traumatic Stress Disorder are decided by a committee of eminent medical and psychological experts who review the criteria approximately every five years to take into account new developments in the area of PTSD. As the criteria are decided upon by a committee, they change all the time. It was only in 1980 that PTSD was included as a psychiatric condition in *DSM IV*.

Ordinary people face extraordinary situations daily and, sometimes, ordinary situations can have a devastating effect. Being a battered woman, being sexually abused, losing a loved one after a particularly painful prolonged illness, losing a child and divorce can be just as devastating as being involved in a national disaster. How many times have you heard stories about someone who has experienced three or four deaths in close succession, followed by an additional loss in the form of having their house repossessed or losing their job? As the old saying goes, 'trouble come in threes'.

The aim of this book is to look at trauma in the widest possible sense. By bringing together experienced practitioners, it is possible to consider a range of distressing everyday events, as well as looking more closely at what has become known as Post-Traumatic Stress Disorder.

The Health and Safety Executive has defined stress as 'the reaction people have to excessive pressure or other types of demands placed on them'. Stress is the product of a complex relationship between the demands a person experiences and the personal resources he or she has to meet these demands. This is sometimes called the 'pressure tightrope'. If you imagine yourself as a tightrope walker using a pole to help you keep your balance, on one side of the pole are the internal (your expectations, values, etc.) and external demands (changes at work or home) being made on you by others or by yourself. On the other side of the pole are your personal coping resources. These resources comprise of factors such as your physical health, emotional strength, financial security, social and family support. Keeping balanced so that you do not have more demands than personal resources to deal with them can be a fine line to tread. If demands exceed our personal resources, we may feel we cannot cope and this is the beginning of what has become known as stress.

Pressure is seen as healthy and something which helps motivate an individual. Some people love to work and live in a pressurised way with lots of deadlines and activities. What distinguishes pressure from stress is that we experience pressure when we have the personal resources we need to deal with the demands being made of us. However, pressure turns into stress when the pressure becomes too great, lasts too long, gives us too little satisfaction, comes too suddenly and results in the perception that it cannot be controlled.

Stress is a very individual matter — a situation which might stress one person may not touch another. In addition, an event which may have proved stressful at one point in our life may not at another, as we may have developed additional resources to handle the situation.

## Causes of Stress

There are many causes of stress. Work can be a significant source of stress, as many people experience time pressures, excessive workload, have poor relations with colleagues or managers, are bullied or discriminated against and experience poor communications within their organisation. They may also be exposed to rapid and/or continual change, may not be well enough trained to do the job, experience a lack of job security and be frustrated in terms of career development. Stress may be experienced in our personal life through family problems, life changes or life crises, changes in our social life and conflicting demands between home and work.

People who experience stress tend to exhibit a variety of characteristics. These fall into four broad categories: behavioural (the things people do); physical (what happens to our bodies); emotional (how we feel); and an individual's personal thinking style (our cognitions). The following are some of the most common signs and symptoms to look out for.

## Characteristics of Stress

| Physical | Emotional |
|---|---|
| Tightness in chest | Mood swings |
| Chest pain and/or palpitations | Feeling anxious/worrying more |
| Indigestion | Feeling tense |
| Breathlessness | Feeling angry |
| Nausea | Feeling guilty |
| Muscle twitches | Feelings of shame |
| Aches and pains | Having no enthusiasm |
| Headaches | Becoming more cynical |
| Skin conditions | Feeling out of control i.e. feeling anxious/worrying more |
| Recurrence of previous illnesses/allergies | Decrease in confidence/self-esteem |
| Constipation/diarrhoea | |
| Weight loss or weight gain | Poor concentration |
| Change in menstrual cycle for women | Feeling helpless |
| Fainting | |
| Tiredness | |

| Behaviour | Thinking Style |
|---|---|
| Drop in work performance | 'I am a failure' |
| More inclined to become accident prone | 'I should be able to cope' |
| Drinking and smoking more | 'Why is everyone getting at me' |
| Overeating/loss of appetite | 'No-one understands' |
| Change in sleep patterns | 'I don't know what to do' |
| Poor time management | 'I can't cope' |
| Too busy to relax | Loss of judgment |
| Stuttering | |

Withdrawing from family
and friends

Loss of interest in sex

Poor judgment

Inability to express feelings,
a sense of being
on 'automatic pilot'

Emotional outbursts and
overreactions

Nervous habits such as
drumming fingers

---

As Professor Stephen Palmer, one of the United Kingdom's leading experts in the field of stress and the Director of the Centre for Stress Management explains:

> Our bodies have been biologically programmed over millions of years with what is called the 'stress response'. Most people know this as the 'flight or fight' response. When we perceive danger our body prepares for action of some kind. The stress hormones Adrenaline, Noradrenaline and Cortisol are released into the bloodstream together with fatty acids and sugars.
>
> This cocktail of substances helps people perform acts of extreme physical strength. For example, jumping over a seven foot wall to escape an attacker, lifting a car to free a child, being able to fight off someone twice our size. Adrenaline is normally associated with the 'flight' part of the flight or fight response, whereas Noradrenaline is normally associated with the 'fight' part of the response. Cortisol acts as the 'on and off' switch for the stress response. Although it is important to be able to call upon the stress response in

times of need, it is also important to switch it off and return to normal once the threat has passed. Cortisol also sensitises the immune system, reduces inflammatory response and reduces allergic reactions. People experience an increased heart rate, blood vessels constrict in the skin and internal organs, blood clots more quickly. Our breathing becomes deeper and more rapid and glucose and fat stores are mobilised as a source of energy. Sweating and increased sensitivity takes place and stress hormones, sugars and fatty acids are also released and blood withdraws from the extremities of the body (such as hands and feet) to protect the vital organs of the body. These changes place the body on a kind of 'red alert', operating at maximum efficiency to deal with the threat being faced.

Although the stress response is normally called 'fight or flight' there is also one other type of response that can be experienced — the 'freeze' response. Here the person may feel paralysed and unable to move. This response has its proper place in the protection of a human being. For example, social workers, counsellors, psychiatric nurses and those working with emotionally disturbed people are sometimes taught that the best thing they can do to defuse a potentially difficult situation with an angry client is to remain totally still, as movement could be interpreted as an aggressive act, which could provoke the person to escalate his or her aggressive response to that of physical violence. When the professional remains still, the aggressor may calm down and once he or she has backed off the worker has more choices on how to deal with the situation — perhaps by talking to the person or moving slowly towards an exit. Therefore, the 'freeze' response can also be seen as a protective response. Although staying still can be taught as a technique, it is also a natural response. An adaptation of this response can be seen in the animal kingdom, when violent attack is circumvented by submissive behaviour on behalf of the threatened creature.

Through his work, Professor Palmer comes across a range of individuals who face physical, psychological and emotional exhaustion by prolonged exposure to stressful situations. The stress response is there to deal with demanding life events. However, when a person lives in a constant state of biological readiness, the immune system becomes weakened and the range of symptoms listed above may be experienced. In severe cases clinical depression and nervous breakdown may result. The good news, though, is that the progress of stress can be seen rather like a bus journey. We may get on the wrong bus, but the sooner we recognise the fact and take appropriate action by getting off the less the distance to return to our starting point. Sadly, some people, either because they fail to recognise their limitations or because the external demands continue to be excessive, continue the bus ride all the way to the terminus.

In summary, the stress response is important to the survival of the human being. However, as with so many things in life, too much of a good thing can become harmful.

In 1967, Thomas Holmes and Richard Rahe, two American psychologists, first published a scale of forty-three life events considered to the stressful. This list became known as The Holmes-Rahe Social Adjustment Scale. Each event was scored according to the degree of stress associated with the activity.

These were then listed in descending numerical order according to the score attributed to the item concerned. Listed below are the top ten items, together with the score associated with each event.

| *The Life Event* | *Score* |
|---|---|
| Death of a partner | 100 |
| Divorce | 73 |
| Marital separation | 65 |
| Imprisonment | 63 |
| Death of a close family member | 63 |
| Personal illness or injury | 53 |
| Marriage | 50 |
| Job loss/dismissal | 47 |
| Marital reconciliation | 45 |
| Retirement | 45 |

In addition to the above, Holmes and Rahe also included: dealing with Christmas; pregnancy; sexual difficulties; legal action; moving house; changing school or college; change in living conditions; change in hours or working conditions; arguments with partners or family; and adoption or birth of a child as additional stressful life events ranging in scores from 20 to 40. Laurie Van Someren, Director and founder of Aleph One, the first UK-based company outside the United States to offer biofeedback techniques to manage stress, recently reported that changes are now taking place to up-date the existing scale. Based on the work of psychologists at Indiana Northwest University, fifty-one events were rated on a 1 to 100 scale by over 3,000 people. Items such as obtaining a home mortgage or obtaining a loan were then included on the scale to reflect current-day stressors. Further research is being undertaken to see whether there are any additional changes or differences according to age, ethnic grouping and class.

CHAPTER 2

# What is Post-Traumatic Stress Disorder (PTSD)?

Most people are so accustomed to hearing media accounts of major events such as the Lockerbie air disaster, the Dunblane massacre, the Oklahoma bombing, the Tokyo underground gassing, the Waco massacre or the bombing of the US Embassy in Nairobi, that they may forget that traumatic incidents don't necessarily have to be associated with disasters. Being mugged, being involved in a minor car accident, a difficult childbirth, witnessing a murder or a hold-up in a bank are also considered traumatic events and can still have the same effect on an individual as a large scale disaster.

## WHAT DEFINES AN INCIDENT AS CRITICAL OR TRAUMATIC?

Counsellors who have particular expertise in treating Post-Traumatic Stress Disorder apply the label 'critical or traumatic incident' to any event which involves the following:

- serious injury or death of a loved one
- serious injury or death of any person
- any incident characterised by experiencing intense emotion
- any incident attracting attention from the news media, including publicity with libel and/or defamation implications

- any incident involving serious threat to physical safety
- any incident which produces an immediate or delayed emotional reaction, over and above the individual's normal coping mechanisms.

Traumatic events can be broken down into two main categories. Those that are person-made, such as: witnessing or being involved in murder, torture, rape, sexual abuse, mugging, burglary, industrial and domestic accidents, hostage-taking, terrorist activity, shootings, hold-ups, road traffic accidents, train crashes, air disasters and nuclear catastrophe. The second type falls into the natural disaster category, such as: difficult childbirth, earthquake, volcanic eruption, tornadoes, hurricanes, forest fires and flooding. In many ways, traumas which are person-made, such as torture, can be harder to accept than those which are seen as natural disasters.

## Diagnosing PTSD

As already outlined, it was only as recently as 1980 that the list of criteria for diagnosing Post-Traumatic Stress Disorder was published for the first time in *The Diagnostic Statistical Manual, DSM IV*.

The manual has been updated three times since 1980 and, at the time of writing, the diagnostic criteria for determining whether or not someone is suffering from Post-Traumatic Stress Disorder are as follows:

1. The person will have been exposed to a traumatic event in which at least two of the following circumstances apply:

- they will have experienced, witnessed or will have been confronted with an event involving either actual or threatened death, serious injury, or a threat to the physical integrity of themselves or others
- their response will have involved intense fear, helplessness, or horror.

If the particular event features one or more of these elements, it qualifies for labelling as a critical incident or a traumatic event:

2. The person persistently re-experiences the traumatic event in one or more of the following ways. For example:

- intrusive and distressing recollections of the event in the form of thoughts, images or perceptions
- dreams or nightmares about the particular event
- acting or feeling as if the traumatic event was *actually* re-occurring, known as 'flashback'
- experiencing intense psychological distress when exposed to any kind of trigger that reminds them of the original incident.

According to Frank Parkinson, a UK-based trauma expert and author of *Post-trauma Stress*, reactions can come at any time and may be caused by:

**Sights**   TV, video, photography, media reports, people

**Sounds**   Police sirens, bangs, crashes, voices

Smells    Petrol, rubber, disinfectant, dampness, sweat, food

Tastes    Food, water, petrol, alcohol, sweat

Touching  Rubber, metal, skin, dampness, water.

'Out of the blue' reactions can occur without any trigger or warning. They can occur at home, at work, in the street, while shopping, relaxing, or resting and, because they have no apparent cause, can sometimes be extremely frightening or overwhelming. Sufferers respond to those cues with a combination of psychological distress and physical reactions, including tensing up, panicking, palpitating, sweating or shaking.

**Example** A woman who had been attacked by a male colleague while still at work, found herself a few days later, sitting at her desk confused, panicked and disoriented. The suppressed feelings suddenly came rushing to the surface.

3. Avoidance of anything that reminds the person of the event is another common symptom. This might range from avoiding thoughts, feelings, or conversations associated with the trauma, to avoiding activities, people or places that remind them of the event.

**Example** Sue had been involved in a caving accident and nearly lost her life. Six months after the event, she could not cope with enclosed spaces, feared the dark and had cut her self off from any reminders, including friends, of her caving activities.

# WHAT IS POST-TRAUMATIC STRESS DISORDER (PTSD)?

4. Amnesia about particular events is quite common. Symptoms may manifest in the form of a total blocking out, or loss of interest in activities. These symptoms may be accompanied by feelings of detachment. Some people feel as if they're part of the world but, at the same time, 'not really part of it', and they may feel estranged from others. They may experience a sense of not being understood and of not being able to love others.

They may also have a sense of a foreshortened future or an unrealistically short life expectancy, typified by statements like 'I'll be dead before I'm thirty'.

**Example** Michael was injured at work when some crates, which had not been stacked properly, fell on him. He was off work for three months and during this time found himself thinking he would not 'make old bones'.

5. Increased arousal, accompanied by sleeping difficulties, makes up another cluster of symptoms. People may have difficulty either staying asleep or falling asleep. They may find themselves becoming very irritable. Other out-of-character symptoms may include experiencing uncontrolled outbursts of anger, or difficulty in concentrating. They may also become hypervigilant, constantly expecting some kind of trouble, or waiting for something really awful to happen.

**Example** Jackie, a usually placid, even-tempered woman, experienced a number of deaths of family and friends in a six-month period. First, her mother died six weeks after discovering she had cancer. Then, two months after her mother died, she discovered her father lying on a floor, where he had died of a heart attack. Her best friend, who suffered from depression, committed suicide and Jackie was the first person to discover her body. Another good friend was given the news that he had terminal cancer and her partner of ten years left her for another woman. Jackie had difficulty sleeping, often waking at 3.00 am. During the times when she did manage to sleep, she suffered from nightmares. She also became uncharacteristically aggressive.

# PTSD

Using the current *DSM IV* diagnostic criteria, a person is deemed to be suffering from PTSD if their symptoms have lasted for more than one month and if those symptoms are causing significant distress or impairment in their social life, their work, or in other areas of their life such as relationships with partners, family, friends or others.

The condition is described as *acute* if it continues for one month and *chronic* if it continues for three months or more. At the time of writing, the one-month diagnosis time frame is a matter of some debate, with a number of professionals urging that this be increased to six weeks. The main reason for this debate is that some professionals report that significant numbers of people manifesting classic symptoms at the one-month point are much improved, or even back to normal, at the six-week point.

Delayed onset of trauma symptoms is quite common. The symptoms are something akin to delayed shock. Any or all of the symptoms already described may surface up to six months or one year after the event occurred — even if the person coped heroically at the time of the event. For example, it is quite common for people who have been involved in a national disaster to appear on a television chat show within days or weeks of the event and talk dispassionately about their experience. Then, one year later, around the anniversary of the event, they may plummet into clinical depression 'for no apparent reason'.

Recognition of PTSD as a medical condition is quite recent. As already mentioned, official medical diagnostic criteria have already changed three times since 1980. As new research comes on-stream, it is likely that the list of criteria will be further amended and expanded in the *DSM IV* in years to come. There are many incidents — for example, difficult childbirth and sexual abuse — which do not meet the current criteria for PTSD, but which still induce all the symptoms associated with it.

### Who Is At Risk?

People often ask who is most at risk of developing PTSD. At the time of writing, there is no neat answer to that question. Trying to pinpoint ways of determining who is at risk continues to tax the minds of some of the world's leading psychiatrists and psychologists. Meanwhile, a number of research studies indicate that certain pre-disposing factors may have a major bearing on the increased susceptibility of one individual over another. The list of those factors is described further in this chapter.

There is also some evidence to suggest that certain changes in blood chemistry immediately after a traumatic event may give an indication of who will go on to develop PTSD. For example, experiments have shown that while people experiencing stress have *high* levels of the hormone Cortisol in their blood, people suffering from PTSD have *low* levels of the same hormone. It may, therefore, be possible to devise ways of monitoring specific changes in blood chemistry or to measure other types of physical reactions following a trauma by using this type of information to predict who is more likely to go on to develop PTSD.

Currently, researchers believe the following categories of people will be less able to cope with trauma. The list includes people who:

○ had a difficult childhood, e.g. victims of abuse

○ have a *family member* with either a current or previous psychiatric disorder

○ themselves have an existing psychiatric disorder, who are depressed or who have experienced a number of traumas in close succession

○ have inadequate support systems

○ are experiencing severe stress

○ have been subjected to severe trauma

○ have a family history of PTSD.

CHAPTER 3

# Common Post-Traumatic Stress Symptoms: Coping with Flashbacks, Intrusive Thoughts/Images and Sleep Difficulties

The following tables outline the most common post-traumatic stress symptoms.

**0 to 72 Hours after the Event**

| Physical Symptoms | Thoughts/Images |
|---|---|
| Shock | Could I have managed to assist? |
| Nausea | Why me? |
| Cold | What happened? |
| Shaking | Must let them know |
| Involuntary defecating/urinating | Can't be true |
| Numbness | I need to call the police/ambulance/fire service |
| Palpitations | I don't understand |
| Triggers pre-existing condition, e.g. asthma | I'm alive |
| | Who'll get the tea? |
| Faint | I don't believe it! |
| Headaches | Intrusive pictures of the event |
| Sleep disturbances | Nightmares |

| *Emotional* | *Behavioural* |
|---|---|
| Angry | What if I had died — how would it affect my friends and family? |
| Sad | |
| Guilty | |
| Anxious | Not a lot of change in behaviour |
| Frustrated | Avoid passing the site of the incident |
| Denial | |
| Relief | Crying |
| Numbness | Behave out of character |
| Fear | Back to work |
| | Being busy |
| | Eating too much or too little |
| | Drinking |
| | Talking or withdrawal |
| | Reliance on medication |
| | Lack of concentration |

## 72 Hours to 6 Weeks after the Event

| *Physical* | *Thoughts/Images* |
|---|---|
| Sleep disturbance | I can't stop thinking about it |
| Lack of concentration | How long will this last? |
| Headaches/tension | No-one understands |
| Fatigue | I could have died |
| Altered sleeping patterns | I may have killed someone |
| Skin rashes | I have to/should have |
| Temperature changes | The world is not safe |
| Hypersensitivity | I'm going crazy |
| Panic attacks | Life will never be the same |
| Recurrence of pre-existing conditions, e.g. eczema | Why me? |
| | It could happen again |

## COMMON POST-TRAUMATIC STRESS SYMPTOMS

Nightmares
Intrusive imagery of event
Flashbacks

| Emotional | Behavioural |
|---|---|
| Angry/blaming | Withdrawing from life |
| Helpless | Overprotective towards family |
| Bereavement/loss | Avoidance of people/places/TV/radio |
| Frustration | |
| Relief | Eating/drinking problems — too little |
| Fear | |
| Anxiety | Medication |
| Panic | Behaving out of character, e.g. shouting |
| | Overworking |
| | Easily startled |

### 6 Weeks to 6 Months after the Event

| Physical | Thoughts/Images |
|---|---|
| Sleep disturbances | Will I ever get better? |
| Panic attacks | I might lose my job |
| Chronic stress symptoms | I am mortal |
| Recurrence of pre-existing conditions, e.g. eczema | It could happen again |
| | Flashbacks of the event |
| Stomach upsets | Pictures of dying |

| Emotional | Behavioural |
|---|---|
| Depressed | Drinking too much |
| Envy | Appetite changes |
| Loss/sadness | Relationship breakdown |

Angry  
Guilt/shame

Change of lifestyle  
Avoidance/phobic reactions  
Isolating self  
Using prescribed drugs  
Smoking/drinking more heavily

Six weeks to six months on, symptoms might include all of the foregoing, plus any of the reactions given on the previous lists.

## Post-Traumatic Stress Symptoms — Six Months to One Year Later

Six months to one year after the event, any of the symptoms previously mentioned may appear. In addition, a few patterns may have become well established — for example, phobias and panic attacks may have become frequent/the norm. There is also the possibility of a delayed onset reaction. A person may have survived a traumatic experience until, for example, the anniversary of the event. 'Delayed onset' is diagnosed if symptoms only appear six months or more after the event.

Anniversaries or events may trigger reactions. For some people, reactions may lie dormant for many years. 1995 saw the fiftieth anniversary of VE Day, which received substantial media coverage. Many veterans of the Second World War became re-stimulated and experienced a high degree of distress as a result.

## Additional Characteristics

In addition to flashbacks, which can also be experienced in the form of nightmares during sleep, two other major characteristics are commonly associated with this condition. See Managing Flashbacks, Intrusive Images/Thoughts and Sleep Difficulties below.

### Avoidance

People may seek to avoid anything or anyone which reminds them of the incident. There can be loss of concentration, a sense of isolation, a loss of feelings or emotions, perhaps an inability to experience the feelings of love common before the event. Many people will avoid thinking about the future, believing they will die young.

### Arousal

Some individuals report an increased awareness of noises and feel easily startled. This might affect an individual's ability to accept the usual aspects of work or family life. Even the noise of children playing could lead to a distressed feeling. This increased sensitivity may lead to sleeplessness, or people becoming overprotective and over-vigilant, fearing that something awful will happen.

### General Symptoms

Symptoms may occur months or even years later, and may also be evident during the event.

### Denial

A person may be prevented from seeking help because he denies the experience is actually happening. For example, asking people how they are after a traumatic event may lead to the reply 'I'm fine'.

## Some Dos and Don'ts

The following are some general dos and don'ts designed to help you cope with trauma in general and Post-Traumatic Stress Disorder in particular.

### Do

Express your emotions

Talk about what has happened as often as you need to

Find opportunities to review the experience

Look to friends and colleagues for support

Listen sympathetically if someone wants to speak with you

Advise colleagues who need more help where they can find such support

Try to keep your life as normal as possible

Keep to daily routines

Drive more carefully

Be more careful around the home.

### Don't

Use alcohol, nicotine or other drugs to hide your feelings

Simply stay away from work — seek help and support instead

Allow anger and irritability to mask your feelings

Bottle-up feelings

Be afraid to ask for help

Think your feelings are signs of weakness.

## When to Seek Help

If you feel you cannot handle intense feelings or bodily sensations

If after six weeks you continue to feel numb

If you continue to have nightmares and poor sleep

If you have no-one with whom to share your feelings

If your relationships suffers or sexual difficulties develop

If you become clumsy or accident-prone

If you find yourself smoking, drinking or taking drugs to excess

If work performance suffers

If you are tired all the time

If you feel that life has no purpose

If your behaviour towards your friends and family changes, e.g. you become withdrawn, overly protective or aggressive.

## Managing Flashbacks, Intrusive Images/Thoughts and Sleep Difficulties

As mentioned earlier, these can be amongst the most distressing of symptoms. Many people become confused between a flashback and an intrusive memory. A simple way of distinguishing between the two is to see a flashback as a complete re-experiencing of the traumatic event, as if you have been transported back in time to relive it. During a flashback, you might experience all the sights, sounds and smells that were around at the time the incident took place. At times like these, people often think they are 'going mad'. An intrusive image or thought is different, because although the image or thought 'pops' uninvited into the mind of the person, the person is still aware of his or her surroundings and can even continue interacting with people around them. This is rather like when you are talking to someone and you remember something you have to do — you are still aware of your surroundings and can hold a conversation, while at the same time thinking about the shopping you need to get on the way home.

## Flashbacks

Finding a way of gaining some control of what is happening to you is the first step in dealing with a flashback. Think about the following questions and use a notebook to record your responses.

### 1. Trigger Recognition

When did my flashback happen?

What was I doing when it happened?

Was I with anyone else at the time?

What was I thinking at the time?

Was there any similarity between anything in this situation and what happened at the time of the original incident?

What do I think might have acted as a trigger for the flashback? (e.g. sights, sounds, smells, anniversary of event, etc.)

## 2. Traumatic Memory Recognition

What memories do I have about the flashback?

What went through my mind at the time of the flashback?

Have I any idea how long the flashback lasted?

## 3. Bodily Reactions

What bodily sensations did I notice during my flashback? (e.g. breathing, heart rate, tingling, nausea, etc.)

If I were to rate these sensations in terms of how strong they were using a 0–8 scale (0 = no distress, 8 = much distress) what rating would I give these sensations?

What were the thoughts I had in my mind about these sensations?

What did I do to make myself feel better?

## 4. Controlling Flashbacks

What things have I done in the past to control or minimise the effects of my flashbacks?

When you have had time to think about the questions, keep a record of all the flashbacks you have as the more you come to understand what happens to you the more likely you are to be able to gain control over them.

A flashback has three phases: the *Trigger Phase* (what started the flashback), *Memory Phase* (the actual memories of the traumatic event) and *Consequence Phase* (physical and emotional effects of the flashback). Your mind is simply trying to make sense of what is happening to you. Although uncomfortable, it is important to remember that these feelings are normal and the more you can accept them the less frightening they will become. Sometimes the trigger for a flashback can be internal as well as external. For example, an external trigger might be the smell of a barbecue (which reminds our brain of the fire we escaped from); an internal trigger might be a physical sensation, such as 'my breathing is speeding up, which means I will have a flashback'. In this case the trigger for the flashback is a combination of an increase in breathing coupled with the thought that a flashback would happen.

### Flashback Log

| Day/Date Time | External/ Internal Trigger | Memory | Reactions (physical/ emotional using 0–8 scale for distress) | Length of time flashback lasted |
|---|---|---|---|---|
| Monday 11.12.00 8am | car backfired | sounded like explosion from gas cylinder at the campsite | Nausea, fear = 7 | 5 minutes did not know where I was |
| Wednesday 13.12.00 6pm | stranger approached from behind | reminded me of being attacked, as person came from behind | Swore and shouted heartbeat faster = 8 | 2 minutes |

## COMMON POST-TRAUMATIC STRESS SYMPTOMS

Once you have begun to identify the triggers for your flashbacks, there are various ways in which you can cope with them. One way is to avoid situations which you know will trigger a flashback. This can be an effective short-term strategy, particularly when coupled with professional trauma counselling. However, it is important to seek professional help to help you become stronger and gain more control of what is happening to you, as it is not desirable to use an avoidance strategy for ever. This is especially true if such avoidance stops you from engaging in your day-to-day activities.

Another way is to group your triggers together into those that you find 'easier' to cope with and those you find 'difficult' to cope with. Using coping strategies sometimes called grounding or anchoring strategies, you can choose one trigger from your list to practice your coping strategies until it no longer troubles you. Once this has happened, use the same techniques to work through all the triggers on your list.

### Coping Strategies

The more you can face your memories, the less power they have. Therefore it can be helpful to write down in as much detail as possible everything you can remember about your flashback. Consider what you find most upsetting about the flashback, and why. Once you have decided what it is that most upsets you, think about anything that you could change about the flashback that would make you feel more in control. For example, perhaps you are most upset by the thought of leaving the backdoor closed, but not bolted, in case someone comes in. You might rewrite this section of your flashback by imagining that the house has an electric forcefield around it and how a burglar gets repelled when he tries to touch the door. Once you have identified what needs reworking, then imagine yourself as often as possible experiencing the flashback in this new form.

Write down what you remember about your flashback, what distresses you most about it and what sensations you feel. Then imagine yourself sitting on the sofa with the image of your flashback on a video. Imagine yourself watching the video from the beginning to the end and rewinding it from the end to the beginning. As you are doing this, try stopping the film, making the image become larger and then smaller, all the time controlling what is happening by using the remote control.

When you begin to experience a flashback, it can be helpful to use coping strategies. As soon as you notice the signs of a flashback, choose an object to focus on, such as a door handle, picture or ornament, and concentrate on its shape, size, what it's used for or anything you like or dislike about the object. Try to keep your attention on the object and your thoughts fixed on it. Alternatively, you might like to keep an object on you at all times, such as a piece of jewellery or perhaps a small stone. At the first signs of a flashback, feel your object, again focusing on texture, shape, etc. If you are sitting in a chair, then feel the texture of the chair, imagine what material it is made out of, when it might have been bought and who might have owned it.

### Intrusive Thoughts and Images

Many people think that the most effective way of attempting to deal with intrusive thoughts and images is to avoid thinking about them. However, although this sounds like a sensible approach, it actually makes the intrusions stronger rather than weaker. For example, if I say to you 'Whatever you do, I do not want you to think about pink elephants, push the thought away', it is most likely that you will have herds of elephants running across your mind and the more you try not to think about them, the more they return. It is the same with intrusive thoughts and images: the more you try not to think about them, the more they return. The most important and the hardest lesson to learn is to allow these unpleasant thoughts and images to come and go freely.

Try keeping an intrusive image/thoughts log, using the 0 to 8 scale of distress as follows and to monitor your intrusive thoughts and images over a morning or an afternoon. It is important that the time you choose is clear of any other activities, so you can dedicate yourself to monitoring the intrusions.

### Intrusive Thoughts/Images Log

| Time | Memory | Bodily Sensations | Distress Intrusion | Accept Intrusion | Push Away |
|---|---|---|---|---|---|
| 10.00 | thought about checking locks | heart palpitations | 5 | Yes | |
| 10.10 | thought about checking lock on car | felt dizzy | 4 | Yes | |
| 10.35 | thought about being burgled | chest tightened | 8 | | Yes |

Once you have completed your log, you will have noticed how different memories or images are more upsetting than others. The less upsetting the image or thought, the easier it is to accept. You can increase your tolerance to more upsetting intrusions by:

- recording the degree of distress you experienced when you found yourself wanting to push your intrusive thoughts or images away

- trying to induce those uncomfortable bodily sensations yourself. Although this may feel uncomfortable, it will help you become accustomed to these feelings and, in time, they will no longer bother you.

### Sleep Difficulties

When someone is experiencing difficulties sleeping, it can help to:

- ensure you have a routine. Have a warm milky drink, as milk contains tryptophan which promotes sleep

- take a warm bath using relaxing bath oils

- avoid sleeping during the day

- avoid drinking caffeine as caffeine is a stimulant and may keep you awake. Too much coffee during the day could still affect you in the evening

- avoid a heavy meal and eating late at night

- ensure you get plenty of exercise during the day. It may be particularly helpful to take your exercise during the late afternoon or early evening

# COMMON POST-TRAUMATIC STRESS SYMPTOMS

- use your relaxation exercises as outlined on page 182–5
- ensure your sleeping environment is as pleasant as possible, not too hot or too cold. Switch off electrical appliances to avoid a 'mains hum'.

If you are not sleeping because of a traumatic event, you may also need to feel secure in your sleeping space. For example, ensure that all doors and windows have proper locks and are alarmed.

Some people find that changing the position of the bed or rearranging the layout of the bedroom can be helpful, as can removing objects such as pictures or ornaments which may seem frightening in a half-awake state. Introducing pleasant smells may also create a pleasant atmosphere. Lavender oil is particularly popular and recommended by complementary health practitioners to aid relaxation and sleep.

If you find yourself unable to sleep within forty-five minutes of going to bed, then get up and engage yourself in another activity such as reading. After twenty to twenty-five minutes, go back to bed and try to get some sleep. Repeat the process if you still have not fallen asleep, for as long as necessary. It is important that your bed remains associated with sleeping.

People may experience nightmares following a traumatic incident. If this is the case, it can be helpful to:

- write down the dream in the third person ('Susan was trapped'), then in the first person present tense ('I am trapped'), until you feel more comfortable with the dream

- think about what the dream might mean. Is it an actual replay, rather like a flashback of the traumatic incident, or is the dream completely different?

- think about how you could change the story. For example, if you were trapped, perhaps you could find a way out or a sudden surge of strength to remove the item trapping you. Practice this new version of the dream in your imagination while you are awake

- when you have practised your new version of the dream, then practice again when you are tired and relaxed and before going to sleep

- tell yourself that you intend to replace the dream with the new ending the next time it happens.

You may find that you have to repeat this exercise before it becomes fully effective. Keep a note, using the 0–8 scale of the distress experienced of each nightmare. You may find that if the nightmares do not stop, they may change in degrees of severity and, by keeping a note of this, you can see how your nightmares are weakening.

CHAPTER 4

# The Ripple Effect and Secondary Traumatising by the Media

Rather like throwing a stone into a pond and watching the many ripples that spread out as a result, the impact of a traumatic incident often goes far beyond the individual directly involved.

Take the case of Judith, a thirty-two-year-old happily married woman with three children aged between six and twelve. Her difficulties began a few weeks after her car was hit by an articulated lorry. Although the car was written off, she managed to sustain just minor physical injuries. However, her psychological injuries were much more serious and she subsequently went on to develop a number of specific difficulties. These ranged from nightmares and severely disrupted sleep to panic attacks. She also developed a number of out-of-character behavioural problems, including obsessively checking taps, lights and door locks numerous times before leaving the house, and verifying the contents of the children's lunch boxes over and over again every morning.

For the first few weeks after the accident, the family rallied around Judith, believing that in time all this would pass and she would revert to her old self. Unfortunately, after three months, her problems had increased in severity to such an extent that the atmosphere at home was almost unbearable.

She could not bring herself to talk to anyone about what was troubling her. Meanwhile her husband, Michael, felt she was shutting him out. Simultaneously, she felt he was not being understanding enough. He was becoming more and more frustrated and angry about what he described as her inability to communicate with him at any level. Her obsessive checking of locks, etc. before leaving the house also affected the children, causing them to be late for school and extra-curricular activities, such as swimming classes and piano lessons on several occasions.

Judith became increasingly irritable and short-tempered and cut herself off from friends and social activities, such as tennis and bridge. After six months, the family was in crisis. Her husband felt he could no longer cope and told her that if things continued the way they were, he would have to consider leaving her and taking the children with him. Judith was also finding it difficult to cope, as her feelings of isolation increased almost daily. Meanwhile, her mother, who had been trying to help with the running of this fraught household, became ill herself. Her arthritis had worsened and her husband resented the strain she was creating for herself at a time when she had few resources. He particularly resented what he considered to be Judith's unreasonable behaviour and he could not understand why she was refusing to help herself.

Almost eight months after the crisis began, Judith's husband reached a point of total despair and sought a consultation with the family GP. The doctor suspected PTSD and suggested that Michael bring her in to see him. His diagnosis was confirmed and within days she was receiving specialist trauma counselling. Within a year, she was back to her old self. The marriage survived, and she was well enough to be able to offer her own mother practical help with running her household.

Judith's story is a graphic example of how both the immediate and the extended family can be affected. However, the ripple effect of traumatic incidents such as the shooting of school children in Dunblane, the Lockerbie air disaster, the Hungerford massacre and the Hillsborough football stadium disaster, which have affected entire communities, is vastly more dramatic. Not surprisingly, it extends way beyond to those not directly involved. The impact on individuals not directly affected ranges from disbelief to fears that neighbours may have been killed. Knowing that someone much younger or more innocent than oneself has sustained life-long injuries can also prove problematic for some people. Thoughts such as 'What if it had happened on our side of the town?' or 'It could easily have been me and the children if we walked by that area just a few seconds earlier' abound.

Not surprisingly, the greater the number of people in a community who have been killed or injured, the greater the scale of the loss. Dr James Thompson, one of the founders of the Traumatic Stress Clinic in London, is quoted as saying, 'To lose one life is upsetting, but when many people die, the scale of the incident brings the whole question of our individual mortality into focus in a much more magnified way.'

## UNWANTED MEDIA ATTENTION

By and large, major disasters, especially if they are of local or national interest, tend to attract far more media attention than incidents which affect single individuals. As a result of massive media interest, communities may be forced to cope with a lot more than the impact of the disaster itself. At a time in their lives when they are at their most vulnerable, they may become the focus of attention on a scale which they were not anticipating and for which they do not have the training, the emotional resources or the capacity to handle. It is much more difficult to deal with a trauma if whenever you turn on a television news programme, you see images and details of that disaster played out before your eyes, again and again. People watching in other towns, cities and countries may also feel the impact, because disasters which happen to people with lifestyles and interests similar to our own may stir up reflections about our mortality and the mortality of those we love.

Even disasters in far-distant countries and communities can stir up feelings of deep upset and revulsion — particularly if they involve the very vulnerable or the very young. The word 'community' can be used for any recognised group of people. For example, following job-related disasters, members of an entire workforce may perceive themselves to be part of an exclusive community. When the National Westminster Tower in London was bombed in 1995, research studies carried out showed that the many hundreds of people who worked there saw themselves quite differently after the incident. Similarly, people in disparate locations may feel bonded together based on membership of a specific ethnic group, or because they share a particular culture or religious belief. In other words, geographic proximity is not a prerequisite for 'community'. If a disaster happens to other members of that perceived community, all those connected with that community may experience a ripple effect.

To this day, more than fifty years after the ending of World War II, many third and fourth generation Jews continue to feel the impact of the Holocaust. For those individuals, the knowledge that millions of members of their race found themselves the victims of mass extermination in a most barbaric way continues to pose a real threat to their community.

To add to their sense of isolation, many Jews continue to live in close-knit communities. They choose to do so, partly for religious reasons and partly because it gives them a feeling of safety as well as of mutual understanding. Like many communities who have been traumatised, they say 'It's simply not possible to understand a trauma unless it has happened to you'. Interestingly, trauma counsellors all over the world report that *individuals* who have been traumatised use exactly the same phrase — regardless of the nature and extent of their trauma.

## Case History

The following example illustrates graphically how the ripple effect can be experienced down through several generations.

In the 1940s, Benjamin's father, Isaac, became separated from his family in Poland and was subsequently taken to England by friends. His father, two sisters, one brother, as well as several aunts, uncles and their respective children were all sent to a concentration Camp in Poland. None of them survived.

Almost fifteen years later, Isaac married Rachel after the couple had met at medical school. She was also an orphan and a refugee, so they had a lot in common. They had two sons, Benjamin and Albert. The children had a difficult childhood. Their father was emotionally distant, while their mother tried to compensate by being over-protective. A psychologist who tried to treat their father many years later explained his frame of mind and distant behaviour as follows. He rationalised that getting close to someone carried the risk of them being 'taken away' — just like his entire family had disappeared. His wife, meanwhile, coped with his coldness by making her children the centre of her life. Meanwhile, whenever the couple discussed the war, they told the children that they must be constantly on the look out for anti-Semitism, and that nowhere and no-one (except other Jews, obviously) could be trusted.

As Benjamin grew up, he experienced terrible difficulties with his peers at school and also socially. Academically very bright, he went on to become a highly successful barrister. Meanwhile, his personal life was disastrous. He married and divorced twice and he experienced difficult relationships with all three of his children. No matter how hard he tried to overcome his irrational fears, he lived in constant fear that some terrible event was imminent. When his youngest son was aged nine, he also started to exhibit the same irrational behaviour.

At the age of forty-two, Benjamin began to experience serious panic attacks quite frequently. Eventually, when he realised that these panic attacks were affecting the only constantly successful element of his life — his barrister's practice — he sought counselling. Fortunately, his counsellor was also Jewish and he was able to help him understand the workings of his family. In time, Benjamin grew to see exactly how he had been affected by his parents' attitudes and how, he in turn, was now passing those characteristics onto his children. Benjamin stayed in counselling for about a year and during this time he learned how to become more open to other people.

To find yourself suddenly at the receiving end of unexpected, unsolicited and unwanted media attention can be very traumatic. Such an experience may be traumatic irrespective of whether you have been cast in the role of 'victim' or 'perpetrator'. There are hundreds of variations on the victim/perpetrator theme. Typical examples of the kinds of news stories which cast people in these roles are major road traffic accidents (where the so-called perpetrator escapes alive, and other innocent people have been killed); 'love triangles' (where a husband/wife/partner has been deserted for another lover); or financial scandals (where someone is accused of a high profile fraud or becomes the subject of a tax investigation).

Among the factors which can make a person's trauma all the more intense is being pursued by the media before there is time to process emotional and physical reactions to a difficult experience. On top of that, the person may be at an emotionally low ebb anyway and may have little, if any, expertise in handling the media.

Handling an interview situation badly can create a disastrous outcome, which can further compound an already traumatic experience. Shunning the media isn't necessarily a solution either. Lack of comment by the individual concerned may create a scenario where behaviour, motivating factors and feelings (or some other aspect of involvement in the event), is commented on by media professionals, or analysed by experts (so-called, or genuine). Meanwhile, individuals at the receiving end of all this attention, who have perhaps tried to shield themselves from media attention and therefore not presented their side of the story, instead find their trauma compounded by having no control over what is being said about them.

Another factor, which can add to the stress of being the focus of unwanted print or electronic media attention, is a concern that any interviews given or statements made at this time, could be taken out of context and could have serious legal implications, should court action follow later.

'Event anniversaries' are a third potential crisis point. A resurgence of media interest in a particular story may revive previously experienced stress reactions all over again. This is even more likely if someone has not completed the psychological processing of trauma reactions in the intervening period. Even watching television news footage of an unrelated but similar event, such as a multiple car pile-up on a motorway, can be sufficient to trigger a flood of flashbacks or other stress reactions, such as heightening fears that the world is not a safe place.

One classic example of media coverage triggering traumatic reactions in an unexpected way was the huge number of World War II veterans who sought professional help after experiencing PTSD reactions, such as nightmares and intrusive thoughts, following the various fiftieth anniversary commemoration events.

If you are unlucky enough to have been traumatised by media exposure, then you should seek the help of a professional trauma counsellor and, in particular, someone who has some experience of the impact of the media.

## CHAPTER 5

# Childbirth and Losing a Child

## CHILDBIRTH

One recent example of the expansion in thinking about PTSD is in the area of childbirth. In the April 1995 edition of the *British Journal of Psychiatry*, a paper outlined four cases of Post-Traumatic Stress Disorder associated with childbirth. The authors concluded that 'the prevalence of PTSD associated with childbirth is a matter of concern'.

Professor Peter Brockington of the Queen Elizabeth Psychiatric Hospital in Birmingham believes that, for some women, the experience of giving birth is so frightening that they feel their own lives and that of their baby to be in danger. In these circumstances, psychiatrists have noted that some new mothers have gone on to develop symptoms associated with PTSD. Recent research carried out by Professor Brockington and his colleagues indicates that over one per cent of mothers may go on to develop PTSD following childbirth.

Judy Crompton, who trained as a midwife and counsellor specialising in trauma, agrees with this estimate but believes it may be very much higher. More recent research indicates that fifty-five per cent of the women in a study of the traumatic effects of emergency Caesarian operation felt that their experience was frightening enough to fulfil the stressor criteria for PTSD. There are indications that some mothers diagnosed with post-natal depression may, in fact, be suffering from PTSD. Both Professor Brockington and Judy Crompton believe that most cases of PTSD are not being recognised.

Childbirth is a natural activity engaged in by tens of thousands of women throughout the world every day. In many of these countries, giving birth is still regarded in the same way as in the UK a hundred years ago: a painful experience that is a rite of passage for most women, that you just grit your teeth and get through in any way you can. Something has changed and the fact that childbirth is a natural process masks some of the negative effects that it may have. Opinions differ as to the cause of such distress being experienced by so many mothers and their families. Is it that women have a lower pain threshold these days? Have they lost faith in their bodies? Do we now have unrealistic expectations of the birth experience?

It has for some time been recognised that there is a social component to protection from PTSD. Without this, how could societies which ritually mutilate themselves and their children escape the consequences of trauma? Our society has undergone rapid changes during this century, as has the social meaning of childbirth. Historically, it was a cultural and social event which took place in the community. Most babies were born at home in surroundings that felt safe and familiar to the mother and in which the doctor or midwife entered as invited guests. Commonly, women had many more children than is now the norm and most girls grew up with at least a sketchy acquaintance with childbirth and breast-feeding. Equally importantly, before the availability of analgesics, pain was part of everyday life. Among the many differences currently experienced, there is a universal expectation of a relatively pain-free existence and childbirth has become a rare event in a woman's life in her community, potentially violating all that is secure.

Perhaps, because of this rarity and the sense that childbirth has been taken away from the idea of a normal family event and, even for healthy women, recategorised as a 'medical condition', there is a move to redress the balance. Organisations such as The National Childbirth Trust support women in their attempts to reclaim childbirth by opting for as 'natural' an experience as possible.

Although many women in the past died in childbirth, improved nutrition and housing, better medical care and the development of modern obstetrics, make rare such an event these days, in First World economies. The medicalisation of childbirth has resulted in the popular belief that giving birth in hospital is the only safe option and that this is the reason for fewer women and babies dying. This is despite the evidence of a female population which has never been larger, healthier, better nourished nor better suited to uncomplicated childbirth. Judy Crompton believes that one of the most serious outcomes of medicalisation is that it may have caused women to lose faith in their own bodies. This faith has been replaced by a belief that childbirth is a highly dangerous enterprise which can only safely be undertaken with large medical back-up teams. In stark contrast to this view, Holland has one of the lowest perinatal mortality rates in the world and a third of all babies are born at home attended by a midwife, with no medical interventions.

## Case Studies

One of the criteria for PTSD is that the person's response to her situation involves 'intense fear, helplessness or horror'. This is a theme which is threaded through the following case studies of women who suffered PTSD after childbirth. For many women, going into hospital at the start of labour is to experience a sense of safety that 'they are in good hands' (sometimes those of a midwife they know). For others, there is a sense of dread as they enter strange territory with unaccustomed smells and sounds, and expected behaviour which may not be clear to them. (Do I have to lie on the bed? Can I leave the room when I want to? etc.) If there follows a long or complicated labour, combined with a feeling of lack of control over the situation, the outcome may be that of the woman whose story is outlined below.

### Marie

Prior to the birth of her baby, Marie was an outgoing and confident young woman with no previous history of psychiatric illness. The pregnancy went smoothly and she blossomed throughout. However, the birth itself was difficult. She suffered excruciating pain during a ten-minute Caesarean operation and, although she was given an epidural to ease the pain, this was not fully effective. She screamed, shouted and struggled to get off the operating table and had to be held down by assistants as the anaesthetist attempted to supplement the epidural with pain-killing gas.

Following the birth, she experienced intrusive images and would stand at the kitchen sink reliving the operation. She also had recurrent nightmares about different kinds of operations and she felt like a 'walking time bomb'. She developed a major depression, avoided contact with her baby and some days didn't bother to get dressed. After the birth, she did not feel any connection with her baby and she occasionally felt like shaking him. Marie became suicidal and remained in this distressed and depressed state for four months. Fortunately, after eighteen months of treatment, she fully recovered.

Other types of situations which have triggered such symptoms include assisted birth, such as forceps delivery, painful suturing, fear for oneself, fear for the baby or being attended by staff who seem unsympathetic. However, one of the issues which confound the ability to predict accurately those who will be traumatised by childbirth is that it is a very subjective experience; high levels of fear may be present during a labour that seems, to the professionals, 'normal'. Research further suggests that childbirth can trigger memories of other traumas involving the reproductive organs, including sexual trauma and painful gynaecological procedures, as Judy Crompton describes in the story below.

## *Elizabeth*

Elizabeth was a young woman who had been sexually abused by a male relative in childhood. After a long labour, she eventually required a forceps delivery. The hospital staff, unaware of what had happened to her in childhood, treated her as if she was over-reacting to her discomfort, while she perceived the midwives and medical staff as hostile. Her husband was excluded from the delivery, but a group of medical students was not asked to leave, even though she asked that they be removed. Following the birth of a healthy child, this woman went on to develop PTSD and decided not to have any more children because of her experience.

In this case, the mother started labour either with undiagnosed PTSD from her sexual abuse, or a heightened predisposition to the disorder. Professor Brockington and Judy Crompton believe that further research will be required if we are to compare the similarities and differences in reactions experienced as a result of a childbirth to what we already know about PTSD. This seems to have been a neglected area; perhaps because folk wisdom states that while childbirth is painful, mothers will forget the pain as soon as they hold their babies in their arms. That is clearly not the case for many women.

### The Effect on the Family

It is difficult to imagine the effects that a difficult labour and delivery may have on an entire family unless it is *your* family. What is known is that there is a continuity between a parent's emotional security and her child's. For example, if the bonding between a mother and child is interrupted or damaged, a barrier may develop between them. As a result, the mother may be less available emotionally to that particular child. It is possible that if the mother goes on to have other children she may find it easier to bond with them. Relationships between individual brothers and sisters could be damaged if one child believes he/she is not loved by the mother as much as the others. Clearly, as in Marie's case, such outcomes are not the mother's fault, as she may still be experiencing the effects of traumatic response and feeling very unhappy. None of these outcomes is inevitable and early intervention in the form of trauma counselling can be of great assistance.

## Future Research

Future research on the subject of PTSD and childbirth may bring about a greater understanding of the way in which pre-natal education and care should be offered. For example, it has long been known that psychological preparation for stressful situations may minimise their effects. Therefore, it may be that if women were prepared more fully for the possibility of an unpleasant childbirth experience, that too might minimise the negative outcomes. However, one of the tensions that exists for midwives and doctors is how much information needs to be given. Some women may become excessively frightened of what will/might happen and therefore worry needlessly.

The role of midwives and health visitors is vital, not just in terms of helping mothers to prepare for a difficult childbirth, but also for the early identification of PTSD. Whilst training is given for monitoring post-natal depression, understanding of PTSD is not generally part of a professional education and is usually only acquired on an ad hoc basis. Judy Crompton is currently attempting to redress this imbalance by conducting training days for health professionals.

Childbirth may be natural and essential as it ensures the survival of the species. However, given the increase in awareness of the traumatic side-effects it can have, it is important that the research of people such as Professor Brockington and Judy Crompton can continue to inform both the general public and influence the treatment models engaged in by the medical profession.

## Losing a Child

The death of a child is one of the most painful forms of bereavement. Irrespective of whether the child dies in the womb (as in the case with miscarriage or still birth), as a newborn, as an older child, or as an adult, parents will almost invariably feel a deep sense of loss and may be traumatised by the experience.

### Miscarriage

Miscarriage is a difficult case in point. For many years and for a variety of complex reasons, society has tended not to treat the trauma caused by miscarriage in the same way as it treats other areas of bereavement and loss. People in crisis following a miscarriage often feel alone and abandoned. Unlike other periods in a life when bereavements are formally acknowledged, the reaction to this kind of loss is quite different. So, at the very time when parents most need support, that support may not be forthcoming. In addition, parents who suffer a miscarriage do not tend to have the opportunity for formal expression of their grief. That lack of expression compounds the emotional difficulty of the situation because, in the words of psychotraumatologist Bruno Bettleheim, 'What cannot be talked about, can also not be put to rest.'

The main problem about dealing with the issue of bereavement and miscarriage is that while thinking and practice in many modern maternity hospitals have become more enlightened, the attitude of society generally has not quite caught up. This is often reflected in the comments of well-meaning relatives and friends who will say 'It's nature's way'; 'You can always have another child'. These comments are designed to try and ease the pain the parents are experiencing. However, for the majority of bereaved parents, a foetus is already a baby and they grieve accordingly. This grief is often unsupported by the health service structure as a whole.

The medical profession's attitude towards women who have miscarried is very varied. In the UK, for example, many National Health Trusts do not offer any form of medical investigation into the reasons behind miscarriage until a woman has miscarried between three and five times. In addition to having to cope with the miscarriage and associated emotions, a woman may have to undergo the medical procedure of a D&C almost immediately after a miscarriage to ensure that all foetal matter is removed from the womb. This surgical procedure is designed to prevent infection, but, for the woman, it serves as yet another reminder that her loss is irrevocable.

### Ectopic Pregnancy

Ectopic pregnancy is another common cause of trauma. An ectopic pregnancy is one where the fertilised egg develops in the fallopian tube rather than in the womb itself. Ectopic pregnancies can be very difficult to detect and are often diagnosed only at the point where a woman has been rushed to hospital suffering from excruciating pain. Ectopic pregnancies can be life-threatening to the mother. Surgical intervention is essential and, almost always, leads to the removal of the fallopian tube. The removal of the tube may, in turn, have an impact on a woman's future ability to conceive. Therefore, a woman who has already had one ectopic pregnancy experiences the worry of wondering about subsequent pregnancies.

The most common worry is whether a future pregnancy will lead to the delivery of a full-term baby. Additionally, the pain associated with an ectopic pregnancy and the way in which she was treated by the medical profession, may be difficult to forget.

## Sarah

The story of Sarah, who almost died following an ectopic pregnancy, is not unusual. During her stay in hospital, she developed various kinds of infections. She was left with painful memories of what had happened and she had serious concerns about whether she could ever face the risk of becoming pregnant again. In her case, it took several months of counselling before she could put the experience behind her. And it was a further two years before she felt psychologically well adjusted enough to consider becoming pregnant again.

### Still Births

Still births are also traumatic for the parents. In some cases, the child dies while still in the womb. In other cases, this happens during the delivery. The prospective parents have been busily preparing for the birth and getting used to the idea of becoming parents. They will both have been bonding with the baby in the womb and participating in the many activities associated with parenthood — decorating the nursery, buying cots, prams and baby clothes. In addition, to go through the act of childbirth only to discover that the baby is dead is a truly devastating experience. For some parents, the news that the baby is dead is known before childbirth begins and a mother may be asked to attend the hospital to have her the dead baby induced. For some mothers, induction is identical to the process of giving birth itself, so as well as having to cope with the physical pain of labour, she must also cope with the psychological pain of knowing that her baby will be born dead.

In the case of still births, the medical profession has, thankfully, developed practical procedures to help couples cope with their grief. For example, if fully formed, the baby will be taken away, cleaned, dressed and then placed in a cot. In some hospitals, a footprint will also be taken and someone may take photographs of the baby lying in its cot. The parents will then be given the opportunity to spend time with their dead baby to say their goodbyes. Again, either they or someone else may make a photographic record of this stage in the proceedings. While all this can be a terribly painful experience, many people have said it was an enormous help in assisting them through the grieving process. Some parents may opt to have the baby buried. For parents who choose this option, the ritual of a funeral and burial, combined with having a designated grave or other resting place, also form part of the overall healing process.

### *Sasha and Peter*

Sasha and Peter were expecting their second child when a visit to the hospital thirty-four weeks into the pregnancy caused concern. Following a series of tests, it became clear that the baby girl Sasha was carrying was dead and that Sasha would need to go into hospital for an induced labour. It was two days before the hospital was able to arrange for Sasha's admittance and during this time the dazed parents could not believe what had happened. The induction itself proved an unpleasant experience both physically and emotionally.

Although the staff were extremely supportive and sensitive in their approach, Sasha and Peter were inconsolable. Sasha and Peter named their baby Natasha and spent time with her. They also organised a funeral service and burial plot for their child. Sasha slipped into a clinical depression which required treatment and at the core of her depression was the irrational belief that she had somehow been to blame. Both parents took up the offer of counselling with a specialist bereavement counsellor. It was a further six months before life for the couple returned to anything akin to normal.

### Abortion

Every day, all over the world, tens of thousands of women face the agonising decision of whether or not to abort their babies. Irrespective of whether one or both parents feel that an abortion is the most practical course of action, they may still be extremely upset and strongly affected by the impact of their decision.

It is usually accepted that an abortion is best carried out as early in the pregnancy as possible. The procedures for abortion are relatively simple and for most women the process takes no more than a day. However, the later in the pregnancy the decision to abort, the more complicated the procedure and the greater the risk. In some cases when the foetus is well developed, the woman may have to have her labour induced. As with still-born babies this means enduring the act of childbirth. In the UK, a woman can only abort her baby up to twenty-six weeks and six days. Although individuals tend to be supportive to a woman whose child has died, people are often very critical of a woman who has aborted her child.

Many women feel unable to tell people that they have had an abortion, unless they believe that others will understand their reasons.

## Louise

Louise was thirty-nine and married to Jake when she became pregnant for the first time. Like many mothers, she opted for an amniocentesis. However, the test results showed that her baby would be severely disabled and would not live for long after the birth. Heartbroken, Louise and Jake decided to have the pregnancy terminated. Although the termination procedure itself did not distress Louise, she found she could not stop thinking about the child that would have been. The couple tortured themselves as to whether they had made the right decision. Louise, meanwhile, experienced disturbing nightmares. She avoided any reminders of babies and even stopped watching TV, as every programme or advert seemed to contain children and, in particular, babies. It took a skilful counsellor, who worked with Louise and her husband for over a year, to help them come to terms with what had happened.

## Cot Deaths

Cot deaths are perhaps a parent's greatest fear. The idea that you could put your baby to bed happy and healthy and then return to find him or her dead is quite chilling. When a child dies, parents always ask themselves if there was something they could have done to prevent the death. A cot death leads parents to question their every move and to wonder time and time again what they could have done differently. In addition, as the police may also be involved immediately afterwards, this can lead parents to feel that others believe they are at fault.

## The Death of an Older Child

Children of any age form part of a parent's immortality. The assumption is that they will carry on after we are dead, as will their children and their children's children. When a child dies, not only are we forced to deal with the individual grief, but we also forced to deal with the feeling that our immortality has been compromised. Another common belief is that it is 'not right' for a child to die before a parent. The younger the child, the stronger this feeling can be. In addition, the circumstances of a child's death also play a part in aggravating the grief. A child who has been murdered, has been killed by a careless or drunk driver, or who goes missing and whose body is never found will usually engender more anger in the parents than a child who has died as a result of illness.

### *George's Story*

George, whose wife had left him when his son Alex was one year old, raised the child single-handled. At the age of ten, Alex was knocked down and killed by a drunken driver while using a pedestrian crossing near his home. For months afterwards, George could not sleep. He paced the floor at night trying to understand how any human being could put the life of another person, let alone a child, at risk. He would spend hours sitting in his dead son's bedroom weeping.

In due course, the case came to court. When the perpetrator received a three-year sentence George was beside himself with rage. The realisation that his son was dead and that the drunken driver would be released in less than three years (allowing for good behaviour) caused him great distress. George had believed in the justice of the legal system and felt the legal process had betrayed him. The stress proved too much for him and he became depressed and was admitted to a psychiatric hospital. With the help of a psychologist, he began the long road to recovery. However, even many years later around the time of the anniversary of his son's death he still experiences strong feelings of anger and sadness.

Tragically, many couples experience relationship difficulties following the death of a child. This is particularly the case if the relationship has already had problems, or if the child was the only focus of the relationship. Even couples who would describe their relationship as strong find themselves arguing or withdrawing. Many couples experiencing such a loss have found it invaluable to seek the help of bereavement and couples counsellors soon after the death, as the counselling process often helps each half of the couple to understand how the other person is feeling.

Such help may be of great benefit to men in particular as often in our society concern for child loss is centred on the female and the man is expected to be 'strong' for his partner's sake. This is often compounded by the helplessness experienced by the man when watching the woman he loves experience distress that he cannot help with.

CHAPTER 6

# Our Assumptions about the World: How Thinking Style Helps or Hinders

Since the 1950s, psychologists have identified a number of beliefs which people apply to their everyday living. The work of American psychologists Aaron Beck, Albert Ellis and Arnold Lazurus has proved most influential in this area. In the trauma field, the three 'life beliefs', which have been identified as being crucial to the speed at which a person can recover from a traumatic incident, are:

○   bad things happen to 'other people'

○   life has meaning and purpose

○   I would always 'do the right thing in an emergency'.

All of these beliefs cause their own particular type of problems. For example, bad things *don't* just happen to 'other people' — they can happen to 'anyone'. Someone has to be a statistic and 'bad things happen to good people and good people sometimes do bad things'.

If we believe that 'life has meaning and purpose', then person-made disasters and acts of cruelty or senseless bloodshed can be greatly disturbing. Such incidents seem meaningless and with no purpose. For those who believe they would 'do the right thing in an emergency', this belief can become challenged when they find themselves behaving in a different way to how they would have predicted. For example, many of the people who were caught up in the fire at Bradford football stadium and the Hillsborough football stadium disaster and who managed to escape uninjured, found themselves climbing over others to escape. This is also true of the sinking of the *Estonia* ferry where many people suffered with PTSD symptoms for many months afterwards. Here were incidents where people had to come to terms with the fact that they had not behaved in the honourable way they believed they would.

Survivors of the *Estonia*, which sank in the Baltic Sea with the loss of some 900 lives, talked about their 'tunnel vision' and how their sole focus of attention had been how they could reach the exit as quickly as possible. Others, who would previously have considered themselves to be extremely brave, spoke of involuntarily defecating and urinating. In their debriefing sessions afterwards, they described feeling intensely embarrassed at behaviour which they saw as out of character.

As mentioned earlier, some of these involuntary and uncontrollable reactions are pre-programmed by our biology. When we are in a life-threatening situation, our stress response kicks in and our body becomes like an alarm system. Either we flee to escape danger or we stay and stand our ground. Either way, it is almost impossible for anyone to predict with any accuracy how he or she will behave in such a situation.

One of the keys to understanding PTSD reactions in situations such as mugging, rape, burglary, hold-ups, kidnappings and so on, is to recognise the undermining effects these events have on people's values and belief systems. People's stress reactions to natural disasters are not as great as those to person-made disasters. Hurricanes, floods, bush fires and earthquakes may kill, but these disasters are perceived as 'acts of God'. On the other hand, bombings or events where human error was responsible — as in the case of Bhopal, Chernobyl, Three Mile Island, the Victoria station bombing and the Clapham rail crash — are all seen as avoidable.

In a PTSD context, the scale of any disaster is not the essential issue. Even a disaster that leaves relatively few dead or injured can leave a lot of people psychologically damaged.

## Traumatic Stress Clinic

According to Dr Stuart Turner, a psychiatrist based at the Traumatic Stress Clinic in London, whose clients include victims of torture and acts of aggression, the impact on the victim is made worse where the blame can be placed with another human being. In such incidents, the degree to which a particular incident has shattered the individual's core values and belief systems can be more important than the incident itself.

Human beings tend to use a number of beliefs to guide our everyday transactions. For example, 'I will go to work and come home safe,' 'If I travel with other people in a train carriage late at night, I will be safe.' When we or those we love are victims of violence or negligence, our beliefs are challenged. From believing that 'I am safe if …' we now believe 'nowhere is safe'. We may find our thinking becomes what is called distorted, which in turn can cause us to become hyper-aroused and hyper-active.

Apart from working with the victims of major disasters, the work of the Traumatic Stress Clinic falls into three broad categories:

- working with those who have been sexually assaulted
- people involved in road traffic accidents
- people who have been involved in violent episodes such as torture, muggings, being held at knife or gun point or physical abuse.

The most common symptoms described by these particular PTSD sufferers are:

- re-experiencing the incident in the form of flashbacks, intrusive thoughts and images. When thoughts become intrusive they prevent the person going about her normal day-to-day activities. When these flashbacks or intrusive thoughts or images occur the person experiences the same emotions she had at the time of the traumatic event

- avoidance is the second most common symptom. What is termed 'avoidance behaviour' ensures the person avoids people, places, sights and smells associated with the traumatic event. If the traumatic event took place in the workplace, the person may not be able to return to work

- hyper-arousal is the third most common symptom. People may be on a kind of 'red alert'. They become easily startled and can experience unpleasant symptoms such as sweating, palpitations, trembling and sleeplessness.

Psychologists have long been aware that the same traumatic event can have differing effects on different people. Individuals have varying degrees of psychological, emotional and biological resilience. In addition, two people may also ascribe totally different 'meanings' to the event. If a paramedic leaves an incident thinking 'that could have been my wife', the horror of the event has a greater impact than if he sees it as happening to other people.

Albert Ellis, founder of the school of Rational Emotive Behaviour Therapy, identified the belief that 'the world should treat me fairly'. However, the world is not a just and equitable place, and to believe that if we behave well we will always be treated fairly can cause great distress when this is not the case. We may behave very well and still be treated very unfairly.

## Trauma Counselling

The aim of trauma counselling is to help each individual come to terms with the fact that the world will never be the same again. Each person has to readjust his or her personal belief system to allow for the reality of what has happened. Each person has to be helped to find a way of integrating an experience into his or her life script and to some extent to modify a hitherto cherished, if initially unrecognised, belief system.

People never forget what has happened to them. However, they can learn how to live with it.

The first phase of any assessment involves finding out how a traumatic event has changed that person's world view. Is his or her outlook negative or positive? Does this person still trust other people? Assessments can take more than one session and involve an attempt to find out aspects such as what actually happened and what the person remembers; the symptoms she is experiencing and the degree of distress associated with these; the coping strategies employed by the person; and the type of belief system held.

### Treatment Programme

A treatment programme is then tailor-made to the needs of the individual. Clients are usually asked to perform some form of homework assignment, which is designed to challenge the person's thinking, while undertaking activities in everyday life which challenge the negative belief the person holds. The aim is to help the person realise that danger does not lurk around every corner. Treatment could last anything from three months to a year or more.

### *Marcel's Story*

Marcel was mugged at 4.00 pm on a summer's evening. His briefcase was snatched shortly after coming out of a local high street bank where he had collected £2,000 in cash. Although physically unharmed, he was emotionally shaken by the experience. What disturbed him was the fact that the street was crowded and yet no-one responded to his requests for help. Marcel had always believed that people would come to the aid of a person in need. As no-one helped him, it changed his view of human nature. His belief system had been challenged and he had to come to terms with his new perception of the world.

## Marco's Story

Marco was forty-three when he went to help a woman who was being attacked. Although he managed to fight off the attacker, the fight left the assailant injured. Instead of being treated as a hero, Marco was arrested and charged with actual bodily harm as it was believed he had used more force than necessary to ward off the attacker. The case dragged on for many months before it finally came to court and when it did Marco was found guilty, received a suspended sentence and a substantial fine.

Marco had always believed that the world was fair and just. This incident left him emotionally scarred as his belief system was challenged by the reality of what had happened. It took over three months of counselling to help Marco accept the fact that the world is not fair and that doing the right thing does not always lead to a successful outcome.

## Arnold's Story

Arnold was an engineer who was extremely conscientious about his work. One day he was attacked by a gang of youths. He told them he had very little money on him, but they could take what he had. They laughed and seemed to get greater pleasure from the beating they were giving him. Again, Arnold recovered quite quickly from his injuries, but he found it hard to come to terms with the senselessness of the attack. There seemed no meaning or purpose to it. It was hard for Arnold to accept that sometimes things 'just happen' and he was simply in the wrong place at the wrong time. Arnold became fearful of many ordinary situations and required six months trauma counselling to overcome his fear that such a situation could happen again.

### When to Get Help

One per cent of the overall population may suffer a serious post-traumatic stress response to a critical incident. Although family, friends and colleagues mean well, they often inadvertently make matters worse for the person involved. For example, they may believe that it is better not to talk about the event, particularly if the person seems distressed when doing so. They may feel they have to offer advice, when it would be more helpful to keep quiet and listen to the story. The person may have a need to 'tell their story' many times. In addition, many people try to self-medicate through the use of alcohol. However, alcohol is a depressant and is therefore more likely to make someone feel worse rather than better. Well-meaning friends often offer alcohol as something that will help instead of realising that it would be better avoided.

There are a range of signs and symptoms that family, friends and colleagues can look out for which suggest the need for specialist help. These include personality changes, irritability, withdrawal, obsessive talk about the event, mood swings, depression, anxiety and a need to keep busy.

If trauma symptoms persist for more than four weeks, people need to be encouraged to seek help from their doctors, who can arrange a referral to a specialist trauma counsellor.

## Thinking Styles

Negative thoughts encourage negative outcomes. It was the first century AD philosopher, Epictetus, who said, 'People are disturbed not so much by events as by the views which they take of them'. For example, if you stood in front of a group of people holding a half-full glass of beer and asked those in the group to describe what they saw, some would say the glass was 'half full', while others would say it was 'half empty'. Those who see the glass as 'half empty' are more likely to be the people whose thinking style lends itself to depression. Those who see the glass as 'half full' are more likely to avoid dwelling on unhappy events, preferring to make the most of what they have.

### Healthy Thinking

Aaron Beck, one of the founding fathers of cognitive psychology, has provided a cornerstone to understanding healthy thinking styles. The ABC model which follows describes how situations trigger thoughts, how thoughts activate feelings and how feelings create actions.

| A | B | C |
|---|---|---|
| *Situation* | *Thoughts/Beliefs* | *Consequences* *Feelings* |
| (e.g. sitting in traffic) | the thoughts and basic beliefs the person holds (e.g. I'll be late for this meeting and people will think badly of me) | (e.g. anger) *Actions* (e.g. shouting at other drivers) |

Our thoughts are *automatic,* which means we may not even be aware that we are thinking them — they simply seem to 'pop' into our head. In depression, these thoughts are very often *distorted,* as they do not match the facts to hand. They are also *involuntary,* which is why it can be difficult to switch them off. After all, we have had many years to perfect our thinking styles, which have become habit-like. As with many habits, it can be hard to break them. Anyone who has tried to give up smoking or stop biting their nails will appreciate how they have sometimes put a cigarette in their mouth or bitten a nail without thinking.

When you find yourself experiencing negative emotions such as anger, anxiety or depression, you can use the following formula to identify your negative thinking.

Another way of describing the ABC model is to simplify it by remembering:

*Situations = Thoughts = Feelings = Actions*

| Situation | = | Thoughts/ Beliefs | = | Feelings | = | Actions |
|---|---|---|---|---|---|---|
| Seeing a friend | | I won't enjoy it and they will think I'm boring | | depressed | | stay home |

Once you have identified your self-defeating thought, you can set about replacing it with a healthy, realistic alternative. For example: 'How do I know I won't enjoy meeting my friends? They have not found me boring before, so why think that now? If I stay at home, I will only feel worse and set myself back.'

## Negative Thinking Styles

There are many ways in which a person can engage in self-defeating thinking. The most common forms of self-defeating thinking follow.

### All or Nothing Thinking

Seeing things in extreme terms, as good or bad, right or wrong, success or failure. We may set impossible tasks and then berate ourselves when we do not achieve them. We may not start tasks because we feel we cannot complete them to the standard we want to. For example, a depressed person may have set herself the task of ringing a friend at 7.30pm and because she is finding it hard and the time is 7.45pm, she tells herself 'It's not worth ringing now.' Someone struggling with a diet may find that he has eaten two chocolates from a box and then says to himself, 'I might as well finish them all now that I've broken my diet and had two.'

### Jumping to Conclusions

We think we can read someone else's mind, believing we know what they are thinking. This is rather like believing we are telepathic and not checking our assumptions out with the person concerned, because we 'know' what the answer is. We predict a negative outcome as if we are able to see into the future and then encourage a self-fulfilling prophecy. For example, we see a friend in the street and he does not acknowledge our presence, so we say, 'I must have done something wrong, he must be cross with me, I had better keep out of his way.' The friend did not have his contact lenses and was on the way to the opticians to get them replaced and he did not see us. However, we have already decided what has happened and why and have acted on our assumptions.

## Mental Filter

A mental filter is like having a psychological sieve, where we filter out everything that's good and only focus on the negative things that have happened. For example, following a mugging, Susan finds herself fearful of going out and becomes concerned that she may become agoraphobic. She seeks the services of a trauma counsellor and they devise a behavioural programme to help her get out and about. She finds this programme quite hard to do.

Four of Susan's friends and her counsellor have congratulated her on her achievements (getting to the local shops, going to the park, going one stop on the bus). However, another friend says in passing 'Oh, is that all?' Suddenly, Susan filters out all the positive comments she has received and focuses on the negative, as if she has sifted out all the helpful comments and obsesses on the one negative one. In doing so, she feels a failure for what she sees as her lack of achievement.

## Discounting the Positive

We make ourselves feel even more depressed by belittling our achievements and discounting the positive things we have done. For example, you have studied hard to pass a driving test and when you pass, you think 'That was nothing, anyone could have done it.' You may have been involved in an accident where you helped other people. You were not able to help everyone, and when people tell you how much you helped and how brave you were, you say, 'not really'. When we discount the positive we take the pleasure out of life and this type of thinking can lead to depression, as life can seem pointless.

## Emotional Reasoning

Human beings are apt to believe that what they feel must mean something. So if you feel bad about something, you may believe it's because you have done something wrong. For example, Mac, an off-duty fireman, watched a car burst into flames and was unable to help. Following the incident, he said he 'felt useless' and then quickly decided that was because he 'was useless'. Here we make up reasons to match events: 'I made a mistake, therefore I am a failure,' 'I did a bad thing, therefore I am a bad person,' 'I acted stupidly, therefore I am stupid.'

## Labelling

Do you label yourself with attributes such as 'I am a failure,' 'I am useless,' 'I am worthless'? Does your 'label' match a core belief that you hold about yourself? For example, Jackie had not done as well as she could at school and disappointed her parents. She therefore felt she had always failed and was a failure. Although she did really well at work, receiving promotion after promotion, she always felt a failure. One day, she made a mistake at work which cost her employers a large amount of money and, following this incident, she became severely depressed. When she examined her thinking style, she realised that she had labelled herself a 'failure' and every time anything went wrong, however small, it reinforced the sense she had of herself.

## Personalisation and Blame

Are you the kind of person who takes everything personally and blames yourself even when it isn't your fault? Alternatively, do you blame everyone else, believing that it is always someone else's fault? For example, Jack was involved in a three-car pile-up on the M1. Although no-one was seriously injured, Jack blamed himself for what had happened, believing it was all his fault because he was a careless driver. As he explained his story, it became clear that although he was driving over the speed limit, he could not have predicted what the car in front (which cut across unexpectedly into Jack's lane) would do. In addition, Jack was also helped to see that the car behind was going fast and therefore the driver also had to take some responsibility for what had happened.

Renee, on the other hand, made a policy in life of always blaming everyone else for what went wrong. When she was arrested for drunken driving, she was angry at everyone except herself. She blamed her partner for upsetting her, which made her drink; she blamed the police for having nothing better to do than wait to 'trap' people; and she blamed the legal system for not being lenient on her. Renee found it hard to accept any personal responsibility for what had happened.

## Over-generalisation

Do you take one event and turn it into a life-time pattern? For example, do you make statements such as 'I always get it wrong!' 'No man is trustworthy,' 'All women are overly emotional'? Do you use overly emotive language such as , 'I *never* get what I want.' 'Things *always* go wrong for me'?

## *Shoulds, Musts and Have To*

Do you fill your life with a barrage of 'shoulds' 'musts' and 'have tos?' For example, Brenda experienced the death of her father, mother and elder sister within a six-month period, all unexpected deaths with no warning. She coped well with all the practical arrangements, but at Christmas she found herself sobbing uncontrollably. She saw her doctor, who had recently undertaken a course in bereavement counselling, and she found herself saying, 'I should be over this now . . . I must behave more reasonably, after all it has been six months since all this happened, I have got to get a grip.' Her doctor was able to explain the grieving process to her and to help her see that placing such unrealistic demands on herself would make things worse, not better.

## *Counter Measures*

Write down your various thoughts. Match them to the headings described on the list of Negative Thinking Styles outlined above. Try to identify which kind of unhelpful thinking style you are engaging in. This will, in turn, help you identify which thoughts are self-defeating.

## Example

'I will never get better' = Jumping to conclusions: 'How do I know I will never get better? Other people do, perhaps it will simply take longer than I would like.'

Look for evidence to disprove your thinking. If you believe you 'always get things wrong', then think about the times when you 'got things right'.

### Example

'I never get anything right!' = Over-generalisation: 'I do get things right, it simply doesn't feel like that at the moment. I learnt how to drive even though that was hard and I got a promotion, I have friends who like me so I have to do some things right.'

Become your own best friend and ask yourself what you would say to a friend in the same position as yourself. We are often kinder to others than we are to ourselves. Imagine that you have your best friend sitting beside you sating the following words to you.

### Example

'I should have known better' = Shoulds, Musts and Have tos:

'Why should you have known better? You could not have predicted what happened and the more pressure you put on yourself, the worse you will feel.'

Talk to people. You may find out you are not the only one to have these feelings.

### Example

'People will not understand, I cannot take advantage of their kindness.' = Jumping to conclusions: 'How do I know if I don't try. After all, I have listened to other people when they have been down and I am not really allowing my friends to return the compliment.'

If we take the risk of sharing our feelings, it can be surprising how many people have had similar feelings. Sometimes our friends have had things happen to them that they have not shared, but which have given them the ability to understand more than we think they do.

Also, self-help groups can be particularly helpful, as the people who run these organisations have experienced whatever you are going through. It can be comforting to know that you are not on your own and you can also learn about the strategies that other people have used to overcome their situation.

Think in stages. If you tend to think in all or nothing terms, begin to think in stages, one step at a time.

**Example**

| | | |
|---|---|---|
| 'I couldn't cope with getting on the bus today. Therefore there is no point in trying.' | = | All or nothing thinking: just because today was difficult does not mean it was a total failure. perhaps I need to set my tasks a little further apart as I did go to the Library and I managed to stay in the supermarket for longer than I thought. I probably overdid it and was too tired by the time I got to the bus stop. I will make getting on the bus my main task for tomorrow. Giving up will only make things worse. |

Try alternative behaviours. If you think you will have nothing to say, then attend a social function and see what happens.

**Example**

Samuel felt he had lost all his confidence since his small boat sank and his brother and best friend had died. Although he had come to terms with the fact that it was not his fault, he felt that he could not cope with social situations. He would fear that he 'would have nothing to say'. Prior to the accident, he had been an outgoing person and socially adept. Samuel agreed to go to a barn dance at the local church hall where many of his friends would be. He was concerned that he would look silly and out of place. However, he was equipped with a set of questions he could ask other people if he felt he had nothing to say and off he went. Much to his surprise, he found the event more enjoyable than he had thought it would be. By the end of the evening, he was relaxed and chatting and he came to realise that he had not lost his ability to communicate.

If you think everything is your fault, ask yourself what responsibility belongs to you and what belongs to other people.

**Example**

Justine's son Oliver was eleven when he started to withdraw into himself. He had always been a happy child and suddenly he became moody. At first, Justine thought that it was the onset of adolescence and, as Oliver would not talk to her and insisted everything was OK, she had no reason to think otherwise.

However, one day, a friend of Oliver's confided to Justine that Oliver was being badly bullied by a gang at school. Justine confronted her son and he confirmed the story but begged his mother not to do anything, as this would make the situation worse. Justine could not sit by and do nothing, so she went to the school. Following a discussion with the Headteacher, the gang was dealt with and the bullying stopped. However, Justine felt like a 'bad mother' because she had not spotted what was going on and felt 'responsible' for the distress her son had suffered. Justine needed help to realise that it was not all down to her. Oliver could have said something, the school could have been a little more vigilant and questioned why Oliver's behaviour was changing and his friends could have come forward a little earlier. *All* of these factors contributed to Oliver's situation, not just Justine's lack of knowledge.

### Negative Beliefs

Some people hold negative beliefs about themselves as human beings. For example, a person may believe he is a failure, worthless or a bad person. These basic beliefs act as a constant motivator for his behaviour: if a person believes he is a failure, he may try to compensate by spending his entire life overachieving or trying to please people. Alternatively, he may simply give up on life, be miserable and not try to change his lot because he believes he is incapable of doing so. People who attempt to overachieve tend to feel good about themselves only when they are achieving, as this wards off deep-seated fears about failure.

If someone holds a particular negative belief about himself, that belief may hamper his recovery when a major life-event crisis triggers a traumatic reaction. For example, a person who believes he is worthwhile only if and when he achieves something in a career context, may find he becomes severely depressed if suddenly forced to stop working as a result of, say, a road traffic accident. The loss of status that ensues could be sufficient to trigger a major depressive episode.

Some people operate from a belief that they are bad people, that they should expect life to be hard and that if people really knew them, rather than the mask they present to the world, they would be disliked. These people are likely to have difficulty in sustaining relationships, as they fear intimacy. The closer they get to a person, the more they fear that person will see their 'badness' and will then be horrified and reject them. Many people with this type of belief become over-controlling or choose unsuitable partners, or sabotage relationships so that they end prematurely. It is important to identify your basic beliefs, so that you can use the counter measures described in this book to change the ways you perceive yourself.

In addition, as outlined above, we may hold beliefs about the world being a just and fair place and about how we would do the 'right' thing in an emergency.

Beliefs about ourselves, others and the world have been formed by the messages we receive from family, friends and the outside world. Over time, we are conditioned to think a certain way, therefore it takes time to change our belief, regardless of how motivated we are to do so.

## Robinson's Four Stages of Learning

Whenever we set about learning something new, whether a new practical skill such as learning to drive or use the Internet, or a psychological skill such as changing a behaviour or challenging negative thoughts or beliefs, we go through a set sequence of learning. This is called Robinson's Four Stages of Learning.

**Stage One** = Unconsciously Incompetent = 'Don't know it and can't do it.' For example, we may feel unhappy but have no idea why.

**Stage Two** = Consciously Incompetent = Becoming aware of what is happening and why, but not feeling able to do anything about it. This is the awareness stage. For example, realising that we leave everything to the last minute because that way, if something goes wrong, we can blame lack of time rather than a poor job or lack of ability. Hence we avoid the fear of failure.

**Stage Three** = Consciously Competent = Having been through the awareness stage and having our strategies in place, we can see improvements. For example, having challenged our negative thinking, drawn up a plan and used a range of stress management techniques, we manage to get a report in on time.

**Stage Four** = Unconsciously Competent = Because we have kept on practising the new skill, emotion or behaviour, now it seems 'natural'. We do it without thinking.

Given that everyone goes through these stages every time they learn something new, it is important to remember that includes you. Change happens over time, and there are good days and bad days. However, persistence and the belief in taking and recognising the value of small steps wins the day.

## Three Basic Musts

Albert Ellis, the founding father of Rational Emotive Behaviour Therapy, has identified three types of demands we make of ourselves, in the form of musts. These are:

**Demands about Self** (e.g., 'I must always get it right') This may create stress, anxiety, shame and guilt.

**Demands about the World** (e.g., 'The world should be a fair and just place') This may create self-pity, addictive behaviour and depression.

**Demands about Others** (e.g., 'You must behave well, otherwise it's awful') This may create anger.

To help you identify your musts and the types of beliefs your musts are based on, write yourself an 'I Must, Otherwise I Am, List' as follows.

I must ..............................................................otherwise
............................................................................

e.g., I must be strong and capable otherwise I am a failure

We call the *must* the demand you make of yourself and the derivative; what you believe is true if you do not comply with your demand. In many cases, the derivative will be your core belief. However, sometimes you may find yourself saying things like, 'It would be awful', or 'People would not like me'. If this is the case, then ask yourself the following questions, based on the statements:

'I must be strong and capable, otherwise it would be awful.'

1. Identify the feeling that goes with the statement that 'It would be awful'? (e.g. anger, depression, anxiety, hurt etc.).

**Example** Anxiety.

2. Then ask yourself, 'What would be anxiety provoking if I were not strong and capable?' 'That would be awful because...'

**Example** 'People would think badly of me.'

3. Ask the question, 'Even if it were true that people would think badly of me what would be so bad about that?'

**Example** 'They would think I was not worth spending time with and I would be on my own.'

4. Ask the question, 'Suppose you did spend time on your own, why would that make you feel anxious?'

**Example** 'No-one would want me and I would be worthless.'

You would then end up with a *must* and the core belief that your *must* comes from. In this case 'I must be strong and capable otherwise I am worthless.'

What you have just engaged in is what cognitive-behavioural therapists call an inference chain. At the top of the chain is your demand, and you follow each of the links till you reach the bottom of the chain, which is the core belief.

Don't worry if you find this difficult. Many counsellors and psychologists also find it hard to learn and, if you cannot identify your core belief but you believe you have a negative one, you may find it easier to seek professional help to uncover exactly what it is.

### Self-acceptance

The tips on the pages that follow are based on the principles of a therapy called Rational Emotive Behaviour Therapy, or REBT for short. They offer practical suggestions and ways to begin the process of self-acceptance. In REBT, self-acceptance is seen as a better alternative to self-esteem. Self-esteem is dependent on the goodwill of others, whereas self-acceptance is the arduous process of learning to like yourself 'warts and all'. Self-acceptance means learning to be independent of the goodwill of others.

Within the context of self-acceptance, it is also worth mentioning briefly the concept of 'unconditional love', a term usually used to describe the way in which parents relate to their children. Unconditional love means that however much you dislike the behaviour of your child, you love him regardless. Children who have experienced this type of love usually grow into well-rounded adults, who have the ability to withstand the idea that they are fallible. On the other hand, children who have experienced 'conditional love' have a less robust sense of self. Those children view the love they receive as 'conditional on something they do' (in other words, they believe that love will be apportioned according to their achievements).

Many factors affect our ability to love ourselves: for example, a lack of unconditional love in early life, relationships with others in the family, teachers, friends and any childhood traumas. It would also be hard to grow up with a good opinion of yourself if you were bullied at home and at school by your peers.

### Tips for Self-acceptance

○ remember that human beings are imperfect — and that *includes you*!

○ develop a belief that everyone is equal, regardless of ability. It is therefore possible for someone to have greater talents or greater skills than you without being a *better person* than you

○ remember that there is no such thing as a 'global rating' on human goodness or badness. No-one is ever *all good* or *all bad*

○ over-generalisation (see page 72) is where you exaggerate one aspect of your behaviour (e.g., 'I made a mistake. Therefore I am worthless'). If you are hoping to develop a strong identity, it is important that you do not judge the *whole* of you on just one *part* of your behaviour. For example, 'I did make a mistake and I am sorry about that, but that does not make every atom in my body bad'

○ remember to work on dropping the *'shoulds, musts and have tos'*, because all they will do is lead you to develop a conditional outlook on yourself. Doing this does not mean abdicating your responsibilities. All it means is that you stop putting yourself down

- remember that self-acceptance is hard work. It requires energy and commitment and consistent work to make it happen.

You will also need to:

- learn to respect yourself
- live a lifestyle that is supportive of your health
- engage in supportive relationships
- set goals for yourself that are specifically designed to improve your life
- recognise that change cannot be achieved overnight and that you will need to keep on working at challenging any residual negative attitudes about yourself
- spend time and money on yourself, as well as on other people. You are worth it!
- remember that you need to take responsibility for your own life. It is all too easy to blame other people or 'bad luck' for bad situations. However bad your position, you *do* have choices. Sometimes it is just too easy to stay in a victim role

OUR ASSUMPTIONS ABOUT THE WORLD

○ ask yourself if there is a payoff for continuing to engage in a particular behaviour. For example, if you allow others to make all the decisions for you, the payoff may be that you never have to face 'being in the wrong', and you can always blame them for the way things have turned out.

CHAPTER 7

# Bereavement, Divorce and Relationship Break-Up

While this chapter focuses mainly on loss through death, it is worth bearing in mind that many of the principles and processes of bereavement are the same as those we go through with other major losses in life. These include divorce, separation, relationship break-up, rape or loss of a job or a house.

Loss is an integral part of life. There is only one certainty in life, that death is inevitable. All of us will suffer the loss of someone close, whether through relationship break-up or death. Loss affects us physically and emotionally and can have detrimental effects on our physical and mental health. It gives rise to a multiplicity of painful and conflicting emotions. It may change the way we see ourselves and how others see us. It leads to major changes in many aspects of our lives — in our social status and in our relationships with family,.friends and neighbours. It may also have financial implications.

## BEREAVEMENT

Peter Davies is a London-based specialist bereavement counsellor. His clients range in age from five to eighty-five, and include widows, widowers, relatives of murder and suicide victims and those bereaved by cot deaths, car accidents and sudden deaths of all kinds. Peter believes that normally caring people can cease to be available to support the bereaved due to their own sense of inadequacy and personal fear of death. When someone dies, his or her death raises fears of our own mortality and that of those close to us.

Most Western societies have less and less experience of death. A hundred years ago, when someone died, their body would be laid out in the front room prior to burial. Relatives would spend time with their loved one, which allowed people to say 'goodbye' in their own way. In the twenty-first century, death is a sanitised experience.

People often feel inadequate when confronted with death. Friends, family and neighbours are anxious to relieve the suffering of the person experiencing the loss. However, they very often do not know what to do or say. Confronted with their own inadequacy, many people avoid contact with the bereaved person. Ironically, at the time of greatest need, the bereaved may find that even normal day-to-day support is withdrawn.

While people's reactions to loss are universal, each individual's reactions to the grieving process are unique. Among the factors influencing those reactions are the nature of the death, the quality of the relationship that existed between the two people before the death and the extent of additional stresses caused by the bereaved's recent life experiences.

All of these factors have a huge bearing on how someone copes with a bereavement. The experience isn't always negative. It is not unusual for people to describe it as an unexpected opportunity for personal growth. Although distressed, the bereaved person may set about building a new life, which might include activities which they would never have thought of doing prior to becoming bereaved. Some research studies have shown that the children of widows do particularly well in life as a result of the difficulties and challenges they have had to face. A death may make an individual evaluate his or her life. In doing so, realising that life is short, a person may be encouraged to make the most of the time they have left.

### Delayed Grief Reaction

People grieve in their own unique way and, for some, the process can take many years. Others may feel unable to grieve, bottling up emotions only to experience them at a later date in a Delayed Grief Reaction. Other people may be able to rebuild their lives far more quickly than anyone, themselves included, could have believed possible.

### *Morag's Story*

This is a classic case of someone experiencing Delayed Grief Reaction. Morag's father died unexpectedly from a heart attack when she was a teenager. A year later, her brother died in a road traffic accident and her mother was diagnosed with emphysema, dying five years later. Morag did not grieve, as she was too busy coping, making sure her two younger sisters were looked after.

She married when she was twenty-eight and had one child. At forty-one, Morag became clinically depressed. Triggered by helping a friend whose father was dying, Morag began to grieve for the first time since the death of her father, brother and mother. At first she was frightened at the strength of her feelings, the tears that would not stop and her inability to block out her memories. She talked of the love and the anger she felt towards her parents, her father for 'leaving' her and her mother for smoking, which she blamed for her illness. Morag had always presented the world with the image of a wonderful family. However, as she explored her feelings with her psychologist, it became clear that she was idolising her parents. Her mother and father did not have a good relationship and there were many arguments when she was a child.

It is not uncommon for people who have buried their grief to idolise the deceased person. Many people will turn the bedroom of the deceased into a monument, preserving the room and the person's belongings in the same state as the day they died. This can be linked to a condition known as Morbid Grief, where the bereaved person is unable to let go of the deceased and may obsessively visit graves, sit for hours in the deceased's bedroom or talk incessantly to people as if the dead person were still alive. This condition does not allow for the bereaved person to live a normal life and to move on from the death of the loved one.

## Dealing with Bereavement

Many people do not realise that grief can manifest itself in a range of physical, emotional and behavioural symptoms. Shock, disbelief, anger, sadness, feelings of helplessness, guilt, shame, nightmares, flashbacks, lack of energy, tiredness, loss of concentration, choking sensations, palpitations, nausea, diarrhoea, muscle tension, headaches, aches and pains, lack of sexual interest are all common.

To help clients deal with bereavement, Peter Davies uses the principles outlined in William Worden's book, *Grief Counselling and Grief Therapy*. The essence of his work is that the mourning process centres around completing four tasks:

- accepting the reality of the loss
- experiencing the pain of grief
- adapting to life without the deceased
- reinvesting emotional energy into another relationship.

According to Worden, it is possible for someone to accomplish some of these tasks, but not others, hence having an incomplete bereavement, just as one might have an incomplete healing of a wound.

## Fred's Story

Fred, the father of three sons, personifies this kind of incomplete healing. He lost his youngest son in a drowning accident. After three years of grieving, he believed that he had come to terms with the death. However, one day while doing the supermarket shopping, he put five 'ready prepared' meals into the shopping trolley. His wife challenged what he had just done. Suddenly, he realised that he was still shopping for a family of five, not four. It took him another two years of grieving before he could honestly admit that he had reinvested the emotions he had for his dead son into the realities of everyday life and the living.

People grieve in different ways. Some need to be alone with their grief. Some need the privacy of remaining indoors. Some find anonymity and privacy in walking the streets alone, while for others, seeking comfort and support in the company of friends and relatives is their preferred option. There is no right or wrong way to handle this aspect of the process.

Bereavement differs from any other trauma in that the deceased can never come back to life. Therefore, the wound can never be healed entirely. The scar will always remain.

Specialist bereavement counsellors encourage their client to talk about the event as much as possible. Thinking and dreaming about it will help them to face the reality. By attending to the rituals of funerals, visiting the scene and gradually experiencing the pain of the loss, bereaved people can help themselves complete the tasks of mourning.

The kinds of practical tasks that help include:

- keeping a written record of thoughts and feelings
- writing letters to the deceased
- thinking and talking through details of the deceased person's life
- thinking about what you liked most and least about that person.

### Unresolved Grief

One of the most important points to remember about the grieving process is that you cannot 'go around' the feelings of grief. You must 'go through' them. Pain that is denied and bottled up is very likely to resurface again when another bereavement or loss occurs.

## Anne's Story

Anne, a childless fifty-three-year-old teacher of A level students, personifies this type of unresolved grief reaction. One October day, she returned from school to discover that her husband had collapsed and died while she was at work. She was distraught, yet somehow managed to get through all the normal funeral arrangements. In an unconscious attempt to distract herself during the weeks and months that followed, her main focus of attention and feelings of responsibility were directed at her students, who were working towards their final year exams. Her way of coping was to 'bury' her feelings of grief and loneliness and attack her work with gusto.

Seven months after the funeral, just after the students left school, she began to feel the loss of her husband acutely. She was, however, totally unprepared for the impact of the loss. As far as she was concerned, she had already dealt with her husband's death. She was, therefore, amazed when she broke down emotionally and had to seek the help of a counsellor. He immediately recognised that she had 'denied' the pain of her husband's death and during the counselling programme that followed, he helped her to experience that pain in a controlled manner.

## Betty's Story

The story of Betty, a sixty-two-year-old agoraphobia sufferer, is another example of unresolved grief. Both her parents were living with her and her husband when her mother died suddenly at the age of eight-six. Betty realised that her father needed help with his emotions and so she arranged for a counsellor to see him. When his counselling sessions came to a natural conclusion, she realised that she might be in need of help for her own feelings. As soon as her sessions began, she started to talk, not about her recently deceased mother, but about the son she had given birth to and who had died forty years previously. It had been a cot death and he was just four months old.

As the counselling sessions continued, Betty began to talk in detail about six other bereavements in her life, all of which had occurred within a very short period of each other. She ended her counselling sessions by talking about her mother. By revisiting her feelings and expressing emotions about each of the bereavements, Betty was able to come to terms with her life. She became immersed in a range of new interests, some of which required her to travel around the country and abroad. In so doing, she overcame the agoraphobia she had suffered from for many years — an unexpected and happy outcome!

What all of these case histories illustrate is that it is important to express feelings. It is also important not to expect feelings and memories to fade too soon. Indeed, a distinction needs to be made between those painful memories which are almost too much to bear and happy memories which remain, providing comfort and contentment. They may indeed remain for quite a long time. Every year is full of anniversaries, however, the first year following a loss (such as the break-up of a relationship) or bereavement may be the most painful. The crunch periods tend to be birthdays, wedding anniversaries, religious festivals and holiday periods such as Easter, Christmas and public holidays, significant dates such as New Year's Eve, and, of course, the anniversary of the death itself. Around these periods, the bereaved will almost certainly experience heightened feelings or tension.

### When there is No Body

Some people experience problems with grieving when a person goes missing. In Argentina, for example, many people simply disappeared during the rule of the military junta and have never been found. The families of the missing have found it very difficult to accept the death of their loved ones. Even today, almost twenty years later, women still wear the photograph of their child or husband at meetings in town squares, hoping to find out what happened to them.

Bereavement counsellors witness the difficulty a person has in letting go when there is no body to be seen and be mourned. But even when a person does have a body to mourn, it is possible to develop Morbid Grief, as outlined earlier in this chapter.

### When the Body is Damaged

Another problem arises when the body is damaged or decomposed in some way. Many people find comfort in seeing their loved one when they are laid out at the funeral parlour. People will say things such as 'he seems so peaceful and at rest', and find that the last image they have of that person is one of comfort. However, if a body has been severely damaged or is decomposed in some way then, if the bereaved person chooses to view the body, their last image of their loved one may be horrific in some way.

## Julie's Story

Julie, a thirty-five-year-old married woman, pleaded to be allowed to see her husband, whose body had been severely battered and burned in a road traffic accident. She felt that she could not really believe he was dead unless she saw the body. Although the doctors warned her of her husband's physical condition, she insisted on seeing the body. She thought she was prepared for whatever could be presented to her, but found herself horrified when she saw the condition of her dead husband's body. The image of his blackened, burnt and damaged face haunted her for years. In later times, she wished she had never been allowed to see him.

Although Julie's story demonstrates that for some seeing the body of the deceased can prove a traumatic experience, for the majority of people such an experience brings peace and contentment.

## Ken and Marie's Story

Ken and Marie had been married for twenty-five years and had three children. Their youngest child George was murdered and his body not found for ten days, during which time a degree of decomposition had taken place in addition to the horrific injuries he had suffered as the hand of the murderer. Ken and Marie wanted to see the body of their son, but were also very frightened of what they might experience and whether they could cope. A policeman who had been trained to deal with just such situations spoke to them about what the body might look like and what they could expect to see. They were also shown some photographs of their son as a way of preparing them for his appearance. Ken and Marie felt that they could not rest unless they saw their son's body and were much relieved when they were able to spend some time with him. There was no doubt in this couples' mind that seeing the body brought peace of mind and that they would never have been able to complete their grieving process if they had not had the opportunity to say goodbye in person.

It can be difficult to decide whether to see the body of someone who is disfigured. On the one hand, as mentioned earlier, many individuals cannot complete the natural, healthy grieving cycle if they do not see their loved one when dead. However, on the other hand, there have been cases such as Julie's where seeing the body may have caused more long-term distress and difficulty.

The final decision has to remain that of the bereaved person and although doctors, nurses, families and friends can offer guidance, it is the bereaved person who has to take the responsibility for making this difficult decision. Indeed, there have been many cases where well-meaning doctors have insisted that a bereaved person does not view the body because they believe it would be too traumatic an experience.

### Children and Grieving

Adults often forget that children experience similar feelings to adults. For example, if they are left out of the various aspects of the funeral and mourning process, they may experience problems in accomplishing the four tasks which are essential for the completion of the bereavement process. Parents should express their own feelings as much as possible and let their children share in their grief. As a general pointer, parents should take any opportunities that arise to allow them to review the experience together with the children. Both adults and children need to take time out to be with close friends and family and to express what they are feeling and what they most need.

Children very often act out their feelings through play. For example, by using dolls to act out the people concerned and what they think happened. It is healthy to encourage children to play in this way and to join in, asking the child about what is happening and how they feel.

Children also respond well to rituals such as writing a message to the dead person on a label and attaching this to a balloon which can then be released into the air. Another ritual is to buy a plant and get the child to plant it in the garden, so that it reminds everyone of the life of the person who died. This plant becomes the special property of the child and they are encouraged to look after it. By doing this they keep a connection with the dead person and also gain a greater sense of the passing of time and of the life/death cycle.

## What to Look Out For

As a general rule, it is important to try and lead as normal a life as possible while going through the bereavement process. There are some caveats, however. Experiencing accidents of all kinds is more common after going through a period of severe stress and so it is important to be extra vigilant while driving a car or carrying out chores around the home. The vast majority of people manage without any help from counsellors, but it is worth knowing when it is advisable to seek help.

The key questions to ask yourself are:

- are you finding it difficult to handle intense feelings or physical symptoms?
- are you unable to control your emotions following a reasonable period after the bereavement?
- are you still feeling numb and empty, or do you find yourself keeping active continuously in order to keep those feelings away?
- are you having continual nightmares and poor sleep?
- do you feel a need to share your feelings with someone, but don't have a friend/relative you can confide in?
- have you noticed you are having more accidents — dropping and breaking things, having near-misses with the car?
- are you smoking more, drinking more, or taking more drugs since the event?
- have you or anyone else noticed a dramatic change in your normal day-to-day demeanour? Appearing jovial and happy, if your normal demeanour is sad and quiet, is just as much an indicator of suffering from stress as the reverse.

## The End of a Relationship

The emotions aroused during a divorce or the ending of an important relationship can be destructive not only to the couple concerned, but also to those around them. The ultimate example of such feelings must be the Greek myth of Medea. Medea was a sorceress and daughter of the King of

Colchis. She was a woman who placed an extremely high value on loyalty, and who met and fell in love with Jason. In return for his pledge of everlasting fidelity, she used her gift of sorcery to deceive her father and capture the Golden Fleece. Jason and Medea got married and for many years were very happy. However, Jason had an affair and ran off with another woman. Medea was so pained and outraged by his disloyalty that she decided to destroy everything which reminded her of her ex-husband. Part of that 'everything' included her two children — her final act was to poison them.

Claire Herschman, a counsellor and psychotherapist in private practice in London, believes the story of Medea is a metaphor for what can happen when divorce goes wrong. Managed badly, couples end up damaging their children as well as themselves. About half of Herschman's clients are men, and her male clients relate just as well to the feelings of outrage and disloyalty experienced by Medea. They also understand the potential damage that could be caused to their children.

### Surviving the Break-up

Surviving a divorce or major relationship break-up can arouse the same intensity of feelings and confusion that people experience when coming off drugs. Those trying to kick the habit of substance abuse often use phrases like 'I can't face life on my own without taking something.' One partner may realise that they have stayed too long in an unhealthy relationship simply because they were too terrified of what they imagine the alternative would be — being alone and being lonely. However, being left alone can force people into realising that the real battle is learning how to function as an independent person.

This means coming to terms with and learning from their past relationship experiences, which may involve facing feelings of shame, bitterness, anger, dependency and abandonment. People begin to heal when they no longer feel the need to apportion blame. The first step towards healing is the realisation that it was the *relationship* between two people that failed, and not the two people themselves. People need to reach the point of no longer punishing themselves or their partner for what went wrong. Many need to stop behaving in an obsessive way in relation to their former partners by working through the feelings of recrimination, guilt and anger. All of these emotions can be transformed. Letting go of the past is the first step to a healthy future, and it is helpful if people can accept that no matter how ineptly they or their partners acted, the past is the past and needs to be laid to rest.

People who get caught up with what is seen as justified rage and hatred towards their partner are damaging themselves. Blaming one's ex-partner may feel justified, but it does not help the situation. Failure, blame, guilt, justifiable rage and anger are all connected with the locked patterns of victim and persecutor behaviour. If people see themselves as victims, they believe they are weak and have been taken advantage of. If they then turn into persecutors who 'get even' and take revenge for what has happened, then these feelings preoccupy them and stop them from getting on with their own lives. Neither the victim nor the persecutor position wins.

## Litigation and Mediation

A lot of people make the mistake of engaging in litigation before considering mediation as part of the final divorce process. Some legal practices have trained counsellors who are able to offer this service, while other practices have links with specialist mediation services. In a few cases, solicitors have trained in counselling and mediation skills and are able to offer this service to their clients. It is always wise to check into the cost of such services, as they can range from reasonable to extremely expensive.

If children are involved, or if the couple is unable to reach agreement on the terms of a divorce, legal advice may be essential. Legal fees can be expensive, as every letter written, telephone call made, meeting attended or minute spent on the case is charged for. Mediation can save time, money and unnecessary emotional pain.

### Learning to Form Healthy Relationships

Divorce recovery work is also an opportunity for an individual to consider how to behave in relationships and what fears or beliefs drive his or her pattern of behaviour. By helping people explore how they function in relationships, an opportunity is created to do something positive about changing the pattern of relationships. As part of the readjustment and recovery process, individuals reflect on family systems, parental patterns and relationships. To form healthy relationships means exploring, understanding and changing unhealthy patterns of behaviour. Otherwise the possibility of engaging in future unhealthy relationships remains high.

### Practical Dos and Don'ts

The following are some practical tips for anyone trying to cope with a major relationship break-up:

- the loss of a relationship is similar to the feelings of grief. Expect to feel disorientated, numb, sad and angry. You may become forgetful and lose concentration. This is a major life event, and you need to treat yourself with the same care and concern as if you were bereaved

- if you are not sure whether you are experiencing a normal grieving reaction or clinical depression, make an appointment to see your doctor who may offer you counselling, medication or both

- try to remember that the Chinese symbol for 'crisis' is a combination of two characters, one meaning 'danger' and the other 'opportunity'. Life's traumas often bring to the surface problems that have been around for a long time

- self-confidence takes a beating during and after divorce. It is important that you do things that make you feel good. This might include pampering yourself physically (e.g. buying new clothes, having a make-over, going for a massage), keeping up or going back to activities (e.g. sports, dancing, bridge, creative arts, singing in a choir, hill walking), giving yourself positive messages about who you are and what you have to offer

- make a list of people who put you down and avoid them. At this point in your life, the last thing you need is people who drain. Instead, seek out people who make you feel good about yourself.

CHAPTER 8

# Job Loss

There are many euphemisms for firing people — downsizing, outsourcing, rationalisation, organisational change, company review, restructuring and redundancy. Irrespective of which labels organisations use, people's emotional reactions tend to be the same. Job loss may also mean a significant loss of identity and self-confidence may be eroded. In addition, a person may feel excluded from society.

Depending on age, personality, family and financial circumstances, individual reactions may range from moderate to severe. The most common reaction to job loss is physical shock, accompanied by some of the classic symptoms associated with trauma — disbelief, denial, anger, feeling stunned, becoming withdrawn, loss of confidence and a feeling of 'why me?'

Job loss is like any other form of major loss and many of the emotions experienced are similar to those of bereavement. In that context, this chapter may be read in conjunction with the chapter on Bereavement, Divorce and Relationship Break-Up (see page 86).

Stress reactions to job loss vary. They may include:

- going into a state of euphoria and making statements like 'oh, it's no big deal really'

- crying openly
- becoming withdrawn
- breaking down completely
- pretending nothing has happened, even to the extent of concealing it from partner/spouse/key family members
- undergoing mood swings.

When it comes to manifestations of distress, there are no gender differences, according to Carole Spiers, an Occupational Stress Counsellor, who specialises in corporate stress management training and employee counselling support to multinational companies and large public bodies countrywide. She says that while men may initially display macho mannerisms, underneath, their physical and emotional reactions are exactly the same as those of women — anger, despair, feeling of loss, inadequacy, lowered self-esteem and, in extreme cases, suicide.

Around the time of job loss, thinking patterns will often tend to follow a very specific sequence: denial, followed by anger, progressing to feeling low, sometimes slipping into clinical depression. The overall length of time a person remains in each of these states varies and depends on pre-existing factors. The most important thing to remember is that, whatever the feelings, all of them are temporary and predictable.

The second most important thing to bear in mind is that emotional shock is a normal reaction. Some people find the job loss experience so overwhelming that they exhibit classic trauma symptoms. Losing a job may bring to the fore other unrelated areas of 'unfinished business', going back over a period of several years, or even decades. This unfinished business may include delayed or unresolved grief over a bereavement, rape, divorce, relationship break-up, or loss of a house. As with many other life events, an individual's response to crisis depends on one's philosophy of life, combined with one's unique survival mechanism. The way people have dealt with other crises in their lives is also an important factor. Personal attitude to change, positive and negative, as well as current state of physical health, play a part.

The severity and duration of reactions vary enormously, and depend on variables such as whether a person:

- has experienced job loss before
- has experienced previous crises which they have survived
- has peer group support, support of a partner, spouse, family or friends
- has someone to talk to.

So what are the practical steps to take?

Depending on how distressed people are and the length of time they have been in that state, it may be a good idea for them to seek professional help from someone who can guide them through this transition phase of their lives. This transition has a very specific chronology, and there are also a specific number of emotional processes to be gone through before they reach what is called the 'resolution stage'. A good therapist helps the individual identify the various landmarks in this process.

## Dos and Don'ts for Families, Friends and Others

Carole Spiers says that the first thing you should expect from people who have lost their jobs is that they are likely to behave differently. She suggests the following list of helpful suggestions for families, friends, former colleagues and others trying to support someone who is going through this transition process:

- accept them for what they are and how they are feeling
- listen, listen and listen. They may repeat a story many, many times. It may even get boring, but keep listening nonetheless
- be patient, be optimistic and remember this is a temporary situation
- make sure they have the contact telephone number of someone else who will listen if they are distressed, cannot sleep and need someone to talk to at 2.00 am, for example, the Samaritans
- expect them to be angry
- recognise that they may feel embarrassed about having lost their job. They may feel they have let their families down
- do not use humour in order to try and avoid the real issues
- value the person and do what you can to boost his or her confidence, as confidence is likely to be at an all-time low

- do not pressurise them
- never ever resort to platitudes such as 'It could be worse'; 'it happens to a lot of people'; 'this could be a turning point for you'; 'you never liked that job anyway'.

## Marriages and Relationships

Not surprisingly, marriages and relationships can go through strain due to a partner's job loss. People frequently find they are unable to discuss the situation with each other and they may retreat into isolation. A man who has lost his job may be existing in an environment of general uncertainty, including uncertainty about the relationship, as well as having concerns about money and financial security. He may blame himself and feel quite rejected — even though those feelings are not necessarily logical or justifiable. A range of contradictory behaviours is also possible. For example, these may include more arguments, more misunderstandings, and a need for more closeness coupled with deepening caring and concern. Equally, a search for independence and a reduction of commitment to the relationship may also take place. There are many variables and none of these states is necessarily permanent.

## The Effect on Children

Carole Spiers' experience of counselling parents following a job-loss situation is that their children tend to act out their feelings through behaviour rather than in what they say. Some children may become quite aggressive in their play or in relationships with other children, or they may retreat into their own world (or room, or self). Children may be afraid of the changes they will have to face, such as a new home, a new school, or new friends. They may respond to the family crisis by becoming quite excited, or relieved at the prospect of change.

Children may become deeply upset at the prospect of change and they may blame themselves for what is taking place. They may believe they are at fault for arguments or communication problems between their parents. Equally possible are scenarios where they openly blame a mother who has lost her job for the day-to-day changes that this has brought about in their own lives. They may become extra-sensitive to criticism, especially if their parents are also quite anxious and worried. Children need to be kept informed about what is happening in their family and they should not be sheltered from the practical impact of these changes. They will experience and feel the impact anyway, and their feelings about this need to be acknowledged by their parents. They will need more hugs and loving than usual. They will need more understanding, because they too will be feeling angry, frustrated and uncertain about what's happening in their world.

### Terry's Story

Take the case of Terry, a man in his fifties who was made redundant from his job as a construction site foreman. He felt ashamed, isolated and guilty and for over three months he could not bring himself to tell his wife what had happened. He would leave home every day at 7.15 am and spend his days in a local coffee shop, at the public library or the Job Centre looking for work. However, he was spotted by a friend of the family sitting on his own in a coffee shop mid-morning. She mentioned this to her sister-in-law, who, in turn, mentioned it to Terry's wife. The truth came out. When they discussed it, his wife reassured Terry that she did not blame him and that they should face the situation as a couple. After two weeks, she found a job with a telemarketing company. Two months later, he found a part-time job with a small convenience store.

Terry's wife loved her new job and her newfound status. Terry, however, did not. He began to feel quite depressed and inadequate. The job was boring and not well paid. He missed male company. His energy levels dipped and, because he was no longer taking regular exercise, he started to put on weight. As he was only required to work afternoons, he started to sleep late every morning and then watched TV until it was time to go to work. As he got more and more sluggish, he realised he needed help, but didn't know where to find it.

Money was tight and the family had to move to a smaller house. Eventually, eighteen months after he was made redundant, one of his wife's telemarketing company colleagues, whose husband was in a similar situation, suggested he seek the help of a counsellor. By now desperate, he did exactly that. Counselling offered him an opportunity to reassess his situation and talk through many issues that had been brought to the forefront of his mind due to his redundancy situation. When Terry was asked to evaluate how the counselling had helped him, he said that he would probably have not been able to consider taking the part-time course in woodwork at a local college. Thanks to this course, he was able eighteen months later to get a job as a supervisor with a small company specialising in installing fitted kitchens. Today, the family are still financially worse off than they were when Terry worked as a construction site foreman. However, with the help of credit union loans and careful budgeting, they are more or less managing to make ends meet.

## Mary's Story

Mary, a single woman in her late thirties, was working as a London City financial services executive when, out of the blue, she was made redundant following a massive downsizing exercise. She was shattered. She couldn't believe this had happened to her. Previously extremely ambitious and very confident, she had not made contingencies for such an eventuality in either her career or her financial planning. Although she tried to get another job at the same salary, there were none to be had. Her redundancy came at a time when hundreds of others with equally good qualifications and experience were in the same boat and making almost identical job applications.

Although prior to her redundancy she had been making a lot of money, Mary had been spending it as quickly on long-haul holidays, designer clothes and eating out in trendy restaurants. Within four months, she was having difficulty servicing the mortgage on her £175,000 home and had used up her meagre savings. The following year, the building society repossessed her flat and she was forced to claim unemployment benefit. This further reinforced her feelings of isolation from her friends, most of whom were either married with children or so caught up in their own careers they had little time to think about her or her problems. Almost one year after her redundancy, Mary bumped into an old friend who had changed career mid-stream and had gone on to qualify as a social worker working with young people.

Mainly for want of something better to do, Mary began working as a volunteer at the same centre her friend worked at. To her surprise, she really enjoyed helping out. It gave her otherwise meaningless days and nights a sense of real purpose. Six months later, when the centre advertised for an assistant instructor, she applied for the job and got it. Two years later, Mary described losing her original job as the best thing that had ever happened to her. Although by now earning only a fraction of her original salary, she was also spending a lot less. As far as she was concerned, the sense of satisfaction she got from knowing she was making a real contribution to the lives of young adolescents more than made up for having to live in modest circumstances.

CHAPTER 9

# Sexual Assault and Domestic Violence

## SEXUAL ASSAULT

Rape and sexual assault are regarded as traumatic experiences. The ensuing fear, helplessness, anger, humiliation and pain results in distress which can have an impact on every aspect of a person's life. However, as is the case with other traumatic life events, the effects of rape and sexual assault vary from person to person, because we all have different ways of coping and dealing with crises.

It is becoming increasingly recognised that rape and sexual assault are not an exclusively female issue. Many rape crisis centres deal with both male and female rape victims. That said, the incidence of rape and sexual assault among women is higher than among men, with statistics showing that two-thirds of women victims will have been raped by people they know.

In a related but separate area, the latest studies from the US show that as many as one in three women and one in five men have been sexually abused as children. Figures released by the American Medical Association indicate that over thirty per cent of married women as well as thirty per cent of pregnant women, have been beaten at some time by their spouses. It has also been reported that a woman is raped every six minutes in the USA. In addition, the assailant is more likely to be known to the victim than a stranger. In America, the term 'date rape' has been coined to describe the kind of sexual assault that takes place when the victim may be going out with his or her assailant.

Experts in almost every country report that data collection on sexual assault is a complex and ill-defined process, commonly resulting in conflicting statistics at both a national and international level. The picture is further complicated by the fact that ninety per cent of incidents go unreported to the police — just one of the depressing statistics contained in the latest US National Crime Surveys report.

The legal definition for sexual assault is any situation 'where a person is forced to participate in a sexual act without his or her consent'. The force involved may take many forms, such as threats, coercion or physical violence. A sexual assault is an act of violence. It is also an invasion of one's physical and personal integrity. International research has shown that rape serves primarily *non-sexual* needs: it is the sexual expression of anger and power.

A victim of sexual assault tends to agonise over aspects of his or her behaviour and often feels he or she may have contributed to the attack. However, the reality is that anyone, regardless of dress, personal behaviour, age or gender can be the victim of a sexual attack.

The first step for someone who has been raped or sexually assaulted is to seek medical help. Although the idea of a physical examination may seem abhorrent, it is important for his or her short-term and long-term physical health. International studies show that the earlier psychological help is made available, the more successful it will be. Seeking counselling at a specialist rape crisis counselling centre as soon as possible can speed up the recovery process. However, many people wait weeks, if not months or years, before disclosing a sexual assault to another person.

According to the London-based Rape Crisis Centre, which has helped thousands of women and an increasing number of men come to terms with rape and sexual assault, a number of short-term effects experienced following a sexual assault:

- shock and withdrawal. The victim may be unable to speak about the experience and he or she may appear 'frozen'
- panic and confusion
- dwelling on the details of the assault, recurrent and intrusive flashbacks, sleeplessness and nightmares
- hyper-vigilance and a tendency to be easily startled
- behaving as if nothing has happened
- obsessive washing and cleanliness, a feeling of being 'dirty'.

There are also longer-term effects, which can last for years. These include:

- mood swings, especially following exposure to events or places similar to the setting of the assault

- recurrent and intrusive recollections of the assault
- self-blame and guilt. Although the responsibility for sexual assault never lies with the victim, many people agonise over what it was they did that provoked the attack
- fear, feeling unsafe, even in familiar places with familiar people
- strong feelings such as anger, sadness, shame and isolation
- difficulty in trusting people again
- sexual problems.

### Josie's Story

Josie was twenty when she was raped by someone she met at a university dance. She knew her assailant, as they had spoken a few times in the coffee bar on campus. On the evening concerned she and a group of friends decided to go to the dance and there she met Damien. They laughed and joked and before she knew it her friends had gone leaving her alone with Damien. He offered to walk her home and she felt safe in accepting his offer. However, on the way back to her room Damien became moody and, although Josie felt uncomfortable, she still thought she was safe. Suddenly, Damien pulled Josie behind a bush and proceeded to rape her. There was no one around and he had his hand over her mouth. Although she tried to fight him, he was stronger than her. His parting shot to Josie as he left her was that no one would 'believe' her if she said anything and anyone who wore the type of clothes she did was 'asking' for it.

Josie lay there for some time in a shocked and numb condition. Finally, after what seemed like hours she heard two voices and she managed to let out a cry for help. Soon the police were called, an ambulance arrived and Josie was taken to the local hospital. She described everything that happened as if she were in a dream. She was medically examined and specially trained female police officers came to talk to her. It was the next day before she was able to talk to anyone in a coherent manner. The police arrested Damien and forensic evidence showed that sexual intercourse had taken place. For many months afterwards, Josie found herself continually washing her body and her clothes and cleaning her room. She was frightened to go out at night and only wore long trousers and baggy tops, taking little interest in her appearance. She also suffered nightmares and felt guilty and ashamed of what had happened. She believed it was her 'fault' and that people would believe 'she deserved it'. Luckily, Josie had a supportive family and good friends and with their patience and understanding and a referral for counselling to a local rape crisis centre, she began to heal. It took the jury only twenty minutes to come back with a guilty verdict and Damien was sentenced to seven years imprisonment. It took Josie almost three years before she was able to say she was over what had happened to her.

The aftermath of sexual assault affects more people than just the person who was assaulted. As outlined in Chapter 4, The Ripple Effect, family and friends can also be affected.

It is helpful if those around the victim have some understanding of the kinds of emotions the person may experience. Many people, as mentioned earlier in this book, believe it is kinder not to mention what has happened and try to stop the victim from talking about the event in case it 'upsets' them. However, research has demonstrated that it is healthier to allow a person to talk. As so many people irrationally believe that what happened was down to something done by the person who was assaulted, it is helpful to continually remind the victim that the assault was not his or her fault. It is equally *unhelpful* to make any comment that could suggest the person would not have been raped or assaulted if they had done something different. After all, no-one has the right to attack another human being. In addition, people may well appreciate assistance with practical matters such as shopping. It takes time to return to any kind of normality and people cannot be rushed. Family and friends have to remember that it could take many months before the person is able to function fully.

Being around someone you care about who is distressed can be extremely distressing and draining and very often the family of a victim need as much support as the victim him or herself. In technical terms the family can be seen as secondary trauma victims. There are specialist services available such as women's centres and rape crisis centres, which offer support to friends, family and the victim. Most rape crisis centres also provide helplines for those concerned about victims of sexual violence. Some run support groups for concerned parents and partners.

A woman may experience flashbacks following a sexual assault and these are more fully described, together with a range of coping strategies, in Chapter 3, Common Post-Traumatic Stress Symptoms. However, it is helpful for partners of those who have been abused to understand that sexual contact may trigger a flashback of the sexual assault or abuse experienced. It is vital that you let your partner know what is happening and have discussed what you will do if you experience a flashback during sex. It is helpful if:

- once you have become aware of the flashback you open your eyes and focus on your environment, reminding yourself where you are

- you think about the differences between your partner and the person who assaulted you

- you choose an object and use the anchoring techniques outlined from page 29 onwards in Chapter 3, Common Post-Traumatic Stress Symptoms

- you let your partner know what is happening

- you wait until the flashback has passed before resuming any form of sexual contact.

*(adapted from Dolan, 1991)*

## Domestic Violence

Every day, women are subjected to physical and mental violence. Although no-one knows how widespread such violence is, women's centres and refuges find it hard to meet the growing needs of those who turn to them for help. Violence against women causes more deaths and disability among women aged between fifteen and forty-four than cancer, malaria, traffic accidents or war. In Britain, one woman in ten is severely beaten by her partner every year and one in a hundred is killed by her partner every year. Violence can be part of life for women in all sections of our community, regardless of culture, class, race or whether they live in a rural area or in a city. We know that many women experience violence at some time in their lives and that it can have a profound effect on them and on their children.

For those who have not had the experience of being close to someone who is violent, it can be hard to understand what motivates such women to stay with an abusive partner. Yet it is an act of considerable will to leave a relationship. Many women have been led to believe that they will be hunted down and seriously harmed or killed if they leave. Others have fears of how they will look after their children. Being beaten and living in constant fear of being beaten is a demoralising experience which destroys self-esteem and self-confidence, making the person feel worthless. The more worthless you feel, the harder it is to believe that you have the resources to live an independent life away from your partner. Many women have been told it is their fault that they are being beaten, as they have not behaved properly or have transgressed in some way. Some women misguidedly believe that their children should have their father around — even if the father is violent. Some men do not beat their children, only their wives, and only when the children are in bed, leaving no bruises on exposed parts of the body.

Some women believe that 'love conquers all', and even if their partners show signs of anger early in the relationship will believe that they can change them. Some women may also still believe that it is a sign of their inadequacy not to have a partner

— 'anyone is better than no-one'. There are women who have grown up in abusive households and have been conditioned to believe that this is the way a man treats a woman.

Women can get caught up in the fantasy of a 'fairytale romance', believing that there is one 'Mr Right'. Along comes a man who may be witty and charming, who at first shows no signs of violence and may be overly attentive. Other men may be slightly withdrawn, making the woman feel motherly or protective towards him. Very often the violence increases over a period of time, or only starts after the man begins to experience a stressful life event, such as losing his job.

### Holly's Story

Holly had been married for twenty-five years before she was able to ask for help. She had been brought up to believe that marriage was for life and the family was sacred. When she first married, her husband showed no signs of violence. However, when Holly became pregnant three years later, he suddenly seemed to changed. Holly's husband would pick faults in everything she did, telling her how useless she was and then, one night, he hit her for putting what he said was a 'cold dinner' on the table.

From then on, Holly received beatings almost weekly and was subjected to verbal abuse. Holly did not tell anyone, as she believed what was happening was shameful and her own fault. Yet, however hard she tried to please her husband, it was never good enough. Over the years, Holly came to believe that she was a useless person. She had four children and when her youngest was ten the beatings increased to almost daily and happened in front of the children. Holly knew she had to get away when her eldest boy who was then sixteen, threatened to hit her and his younger sister with the words: 'Dad knows how to get what he wants!' A daytime chat show featuring the stories of abused women provided a helpline number which Holly rang, and within two days she had packed her bags and had moved herself and three of the children to a women's refuge many miles away. Sadly, she knew that her eldest boy would not leave his father and would in any case, as soon as he could, make contact with him. Holly therefore left him behind, a decision which was hard to make.

Away from the violence, she and the children began to suffer a range of symptoms associated with trauma. Holly could not sleep, felt extremely anxious most of the time, suffered a range of stress-related physical ailments and became almost agoraphobic. Her children, too, found it hard to settle and a range of behavioural problems ensued. Two of her children started bed-wetting. Holly now believed she had done the wrong thing and it took all the skills of a counsellor to help her understand that now she was safe, she was able to experience all the feelings that she had been bottling up for so long. The analogy the counsellor used was that of war. When you are in the front-line, survival is all you think about and it is only when you are safe that you can truly think about what has happened to you.

Holly and her children also received family therapy and it took almost a year before they felt able to cope with everyday life. Holly was finally offered a council flat and she attended a local training scheme. She soon found that she was a capable person and she and her family were able to make a new life. In time, she even managed to start divorce proceedings against her husband.

Typical feelings associated with domestic violence are:

- a sense of worthlessness
- fear of when the next beating will happen
- shame that this is happening
- misguided beliefs that children need their father
- feeling guilty when friends and family tell you should leave.

Many women who escape violent relationships manifest the same symptoms as soldiers returning from a battlefield and counsellors use the same techniques as in trauma counselling to help them. When a woman has been beaten, tortured and made to feel she is nothing, it can take many months of painstaking work to help her face her past, come to terms with her present and plan for her future.

Children who have either experienced or witnessed violence are also often traumatised. Even a very young child can be frightened by the sounds and sights they experience. Such children may develop a range of behavioural difficulties and anxiety-related disorders. As the child grows, he or she may develop in one of two ways. Some children take on the characteristics of the abuser and become aggressive to those around them. In adult life, they are likely to become the aggressor and, if male, more likely to abuse their partners. Others, usually females, can become passive and fearful of confrontation. Such women are likely to have a series of unsuccessful relationships where they are abused in some way. Abuse can take many forms, and even if they are not physically abused, they may well form relationships with men who verbally and emotionally abuse them. In these cases, a woman may feel that she has done well to avoid a physically abusive partner and not realise that she is suffering other forms of abuse. In both cases, the conditioning factors of early life have taken their toll. Not surprisingly, this group of women have difficulty in expressing anger and exhibit passive behaviour.

Although research on men is less specific, it now appears that a number of men are emerging from violent relationships and manifest all the symptoms above. However, many men feel that society does not believe them when they claim to have been 'battered', even where they have a history of hospital appointments for a series of broken bones behind them. Female violence is a new concept and one about which we will be hearing more in the future.

CHAPTER 10

# The Cost of Caring — Prolonged Duress Stress Disorder (PDSD)

One of the most neglected areas of thinking in the trauma field is that of the emotional, physical and psychological pressures experienced by those who care for loved ones. In the UK, carers already account for almost one in seven of the adult population. This ratio is alarmingly high and figures are set to increase even further in the next ten years. This is as a result of demographic changes in most of the European Union Member States as well as in the US and other First World countries. The world is experiencing a so-called 'greying of the population' phenomenon, as people live to much older ages than ever before.

Perhaps even more alarming is the increase in carers who are children. Many young people now carry the responsibility of managing a house, shopping, cooking and cleaning on top of their schooling. In addition, the eldest child in a family maybe responsible for the day-to-day well-being of younger siblings. Many are unable to engage in normal childhood or adolescent activities, due to the responsibilities they hold. This is particulary true in one-parent families. As well as the practical responsibilities such caring brings, many young people who have been carers from an early age go on to develop an overly responsible attitude towards life. They may know no other role than that of the carer, and therefore find themselves engaging in relationships which require them to become the carer, as this is a role they feel comfortable with. Alternatively, a small percentage go on to avoid the intimacy of close relationships, in later life, fearing that they will be called upon to look after a partner. This may mean facing a string of unfulfilling relationships, ending in separation or divorce.

Caring for someone can be physically exhausting and emotionally draining. Many carers may be elderly themselves and have great difficulty looking after parents or relatives who could not otherwise manage without help. In addition, a significant number of carers have devoted their lives to looking after relatives, which can cause loneliness and despair when relatives die, leaving the carer alone in the world.

Working as a carer is unpaid and brings no status or contract of employment. Many give up employment or reduce their hours in order to take on full-time caring roles. As a result, they miss out on job opportunities and face the prospect of financial hardship, because they have no chance to build up savings or a pension. The many other stresses they have to deal with include having to witness loved ones deteriorate and change. Dementia is a particularly distressing case in point. In such instances, the patient may not recognise their carer, they may soil themselves and become abusive and violent. Meantime, the carer may be suffering from lack of sleep, whilst trying to come to terms with the fact that the person they loved is no longer available to them emotionally. Over a period of time, they may experience a severe stress response, including tiredness and an inability to cope.

## PDSD AND CARING

Some people develop symptoms normally associated with PTSD following caring for a loved one.

### Julie's Story

Julie was forty when she gave up work to look after her elderly parents. Her father died a year later from a heart attack and her mother, then eighty-nine, developed dementia following a series of small strokes. Caring for her mother was a full-time job due to her physical disability, and so Julie's contact with the outside world diminished. Her mother deteriorated and was unable to recognise Julie as her daughter. Instead, she was convinced she was someone who had evil intentions towards her. Her mother would scream at Julie and then proceed to cry for the daughter, whom she believed 'the evil person' had taken away.

The next major blow for Julie was when her mother was diagnosed with terminal cancer. However, instead of a swift death, she was forced to watch helplessly as the person she felt closest to in the entire world died, without dignity, over an eighteen-month period, suffering from the distressing and totally disabling conditions of dementia and cancer combined. When the end finally came, following many false alarms and all-night vigils around her bedside, Julie went to pieces. She developed panic attacks, became phobic about dying and suffered from intrusive thoughts and images of her mother's death. She would avoid any television or radio programme featuring medical topics and refused to go to her doctor, even though she needed treatment. She withdrew even further into herself, only ever venturing out into the world for essential items such as food. One day, Julie reached for the telephone and rang a local counselling agency.

Luckily, the person she spoke to was able to offer Julie a home visit and this was the start of her recovery. When she was clinically assessed by a counsellor, it became clear that all her symptoms were those associated with PTSD. Although the activating event would not qualify under the current diagnostic criteria (see reference to *DSM IV*, page 12), the counsellor put Julie on a PTSD counselling programme. Within a year, she had returned to her old job as a book keeper and she was no longer plagued by panic attacks and other symptoms.

### The Young Carer

An example of what can happen to a young carer is the case of Miguel.

### *Miguel's Story*

Miguel was seven when his mother developed multiple sclerosis, a degenerative disease of the nervous system. For some people, it may take twenty years before they become severely disabled by the disease and for others only a few years. In Miguel's case, his mother's illness progressed quickly and by the time he was eleven she was in a wheelchair, had partial speech and had lost forty-five per cent use of her arms. Miguel was an only child who had no contact with his father, who had left when his mother was pregnant. Miguel had to learn to take care of both his mother and himself from an early age. He cooked, cleaned, did the shopping, ran errands and had little time to socialise with friends from school. Although

Miguel loved his mother, he was also ashamed to have friends come and visit. He got to go out with his friends only on an irregular basis and spent most of his time with his mother. Although Social Services arranged for a home help to attend and would from time to time arrange respite care for his mother, Miguel had very little support. In addition — like so many child carers — he also lived in fear that his mother would be taken away and he would be sent to a home or to foster care.

Miguel's mother died when he was seventeen. He was allowed to stay in the Council flat he and his mother had lived in and he started a government training scheme. By twenty he was working in an office, but would tend to be quiet and solitary. At twenty-two he had his first girlfriend, whom he later married. However, he never allowed her to get too close to him and he became extremely anxious when she became pregnant. He developed panic attacks and had nightmares of watching his mother's body contort. His doctor signed him off work and arranged for him to receive counselling. Through the counselling, Miguel was able to explore his fears of being trapped by having a 'wife and child to look after', his fears of illness, his love and also his anger at his mother for his lost childhood and his difficulties in allowing himself to get close to anyone. After twelve counselling sessions, Miguel's anxiety had abated and he and his wife went on to a further twelve sessions of couples counselling to help them improve their relationship. Miguel was able to return to work, his relationship improved and he enjoyed being a father.

## Recognising PDSD

Not surprisingly, given the close similarity between the two acronyms, PTSD and PDSD are often confused. The physical and psychological manifestations of Prolonged Duress Stress Disorder and Post-Traumatic Stress Disorder, are, however, quite different. In order to be diagnosed legitimately as suffering from PTSD, the criteria laid down in *DSM IV* (see page 12) must be met. That is not to say that PDSD is not a legitimate condition in its own right. It is. However, in terms of classification, it is quite different.

PDSD is a common reaction amongst groups such as carers of the chronically or terminally ill or parents who care for children with severe physical and mental disabilities. PDSD sufferers also include people who are exposed to cumulative stress in their lives, as a result of having had to deal with situations such as child sexual abuse, domestic violence, family desertion, homelessness, long-term involuntary unemployment or other huge life- event difficulties beyond their personal control.

Being forced to deal long term with people who have psychiatric problems or serious personality disorders can also lead to PDSD.

The disorder is also common among victims of man-made famines, as well as among victims of refugee crises and racism. Even those who are paid to help, such as counsellors, psychologists, social workers, doctors and nurses, can be affected. There are many documented cases of PDSD among Third World relief agency workers and among housing officers and other officials who help on a professional basis. The greater the inability to solve a series of ongoing crises or someone else's needs, the greater the chances of developing PDSD. In fact, if the circumstances are severe and sustained over a long enough period, such workers may end up suffering from a stress-related condition called 'burn out'.

As was mentioned in the early pages of this book, 'your biology doesn't read the *DSM IV* manual' — it just reacts to what is happening. You will know you are in need of help from a trauma counsellor if you display the following symptoms:

- you are no longer able to function on a daily basis without getting upset
- you are tearful
- you experience four or more of the symptoms on the Depression checklist (see page 164)
- your coping skills desert you
- you have to take time off work for extended periods
- you suddenly become phobic about certain places, people or situations.

In many cases, the traumatic incident may be 'the last straw', leading to an Acute Stress Reaction or PDSD with the symptoms associated with PTSD in *DSM IV*. The trigger may be as trivial as someone shouting at you, someone making a demand or a mild personality clash in a work environment. As explained earlier in Chapter 1, Understanding Trauma and Stress, the accumulation of stress can be seen in terms of 'a dripping tap', where just one extra drop leads to the whole system overflowing.

## Petra's Story

Petra worked as a housing officer for an inner-city local authority. For five years her department underwent constant reorganisation. Some of her colleagues had been made redundant during this time and she lived with the uncertainty of losing her own job. A new manager had been appointed and for the past two years had been very critical of her work, for no apparent reason. Most of her friends had left the office; those that remained seemed less supportive and kept to themselves. New directives were issued frequently and each one increased Petra's workload. The degree of daily abuse by tenants also increased. She ran into financial difficulties following the break-up of a long-term relationship. Her eldest child was hyperactive and difficult to control. Her ex-partner refused to provide maintenance or help with the children. Petra had also become a diabetic. She sometimes wondered how she managed to keep going: each day seemed a struggle.

One day, a tenant threatened to 'smash her face in' and, although such comments were a daily occurrence, she fell to pieces. This threat was the last straw. She was sent home as unfit for work. She suffered panic attacks, became agoraphobic, and displayed a whole range of emotional, physical and psychological symptoms. She visited her doctor who referred her to the counsellor at his practice. After assessment, it was evident that Petra was experiencing a range of symptoms associated with PTSD. In her case, the build-up of stressful events over a period of time had led to PDSD. A three-month course of counselling enabled Petra to return to work and to manage her situation more effectively.

## CHAPTER 11

# Cults

The psychological effect of being involved in a cult is an area people do not normally associate with Post-Traumatic Stress Disorder. Living in a restrictive community isolated from the rest of the world can create serious long-term stress reactions in several different ways.

### A 'Living Death'

Jill Mytton, a Chartered Psychologist and Senior Lecturer at the University of East London who specialises in working with ex-cult members, talks about the 'death of personality' or 'murder of the soul' which derives from the cumulative effect of not being allowed to 'be yourself'. If people are brought up in a cult, they are told what to think, how to behave and what to feel. Meanwhile, all the other aspects of a person's day-to-day life are also prescribed by the culture of the cult. The structure of a cult revolves around keeping an individual enclosed within the confines of the cult. A variety of techniques are used to keep members within the cult.

#### Sarah's Story

Sarah was brought up in a middle-class family in a big town several hundred miles north of London. Her parents had first met at a sect bible reading. They were strict followers of that sect and insisted that each of the five children born into the marriage should follow its codes and practices. Their third child had different ideas. When she reached the age of eighteen, she decided that for the sake of her future mental survival she would have to break away from the suffocation of sect and family life combined.

Daily life at home was oppressive, yet Sarah knew that raising doubts about her family's beliefs and way of life was out of the question. She also knew that they would not let her escape into the outside world willingly. Such were her fears about her family's reaction that she eventually sneaked away from home in the dead of night. She took nothing with her, other than £150 she had managed to save over a two-and-a-half year period, and made her way to London. Unusually for someone without any formal training, she got a job fairly quickly after she spotted an advertisement in a tube station for telesales operators. The job paid fairly well. However, staff turnover and the daily pressures of the work did not leave time to engage in social chit-chat with her work colleagues.

Sarah liked the anonymity of the job and revelled in her freedom. She even experimented with boyfriends for the first time. She was relieved at having escaped from her family and the religious sect to which they belonged, but remained quite anxious that she would be 'recaptured'. For two years she remained out of contact with her family. However, she also missed her family and one weekend she turned up at her former home unannounced. The family's reaction to the return of their prodigal daughter was swift and brutal. She was incarcerated in the house for six weeks, during which time her sole contact was with her hostile family and several equally hostile sect members while she was locked in her room. This six-week period was marked by a number of traumatic incidents, including several sessions where she was bombarded with questions and was forced to undergo a public confession of everything she had done during the time she had been away from the sect. This included revealing the most minute details of her sexual encounters.

Eventually, Sarah managed to escape a second time in the dead of night. This time she sought the help of the Samaritans, who in turn put her in touch with the Cults Information Centre, who put her in touch with Catalyst, a London-based self-help group, who organised trauma counselling for her.

One of the things Sarah talked about during those trauma counselling sessions was how a lifetime of sect indoctrination had taught her to regard every culture other than its own as evil, wicked, unsafe and alien. During her first few weeks of freedom, simple things like ordering a meal in a café on her own posed a huge challenge. Much more traumatic was learning through an intermediary that her father was ill in hospital. She tracked down the name of the hospital and she discovered her father had cancer. However, when she phoned the ward to find out how he was, the nurses informed her that the family had given explicit instructions not to reveal any information whatsoever to this wayward daughter. Telephone calls to her mother, brothers and sisters proved equally fruitless. Sarah then had to come to terms with the fact that if her father died, she would not be informed, and that her family had totally disowned her. Many months of counselling and specialist support were needed to help Sarah rebuild her life, come to terms with her past and, in particular, the traumas of the hostage situation she escaped from and the fact that she was now an 'orphan', cut off from her family probably for the rest of her life.

This type of 'family withholding information', or 'family disowning ex-cult member' scenario is by no means unusual. There are countless examples of men and women whose families have done this and worse. A process not dissimilar to that associated with grieving is likely to ensue following the loss of contact with close family members. Ex-cult members describe this situation as a 'living death'.

One of the problems in trying to help ex-cult members is that their stress reactions tend to be so severe that even talking about their experience is overwhelmingly distressing. In addition, they will invariably have been brainwashed or indoctrinated not to reveal details of the hierarchies, activities and workings of the particular sect they belonged to.

## Cults and PTSD

In a recent study of more than 200 former members of one particular fundamentalist sect, Jill Mytton found that an estimated sixty per cent were suffering from some of the classic symptoms of PTSD, such as nightmares, intrusive thoughts and avoidance of situations reminding them of the sect. About fifteen per cent would probably be diagnosed with full-blown PTSD except that according to the current *DSM IV* diagnosis, they do not satisfy the criteria with regards to the events that qualify as traumatic. Jill herself left the sect over thirty years ago, yet still occasionally has nightmares and intrusive thoughts, despite trauma counselling. The former members she studied reported common problems, such as difficulty making decisions and tolerating ambiguity. Another common feature is finding it difficult to feel part of a group – *any* group. Jill has had more than fifteen years' experience helping former cult members adjust to their new lives as 'aliens in their own country'. Amongst other things, she has set up an email support group for former members and has contributed to a website set up by a former member in the USA. She advises anyone unlucky enough to find themselves traumatised by current or previous membership of a cult to contact groups like the Cult Information Centre and Catalyst (see pages 197 and 199 for further details). Organisations like these can help put those in need of help in touch with an appropriately qualified trauma counsellor.

For those interested in gaining insights into the way cults manipulate and indoctrinate their members, Jill recommends a book called *Captive Hearts, Captive Minds: Freedom and Recovery from Cults and Abusive Relationships* (see page 208 for further details).

CHAPTER 12

# Critical Incident Stress Debriefing and Emergency Services Personnel and Trauma

One of the options available to people who have either witnessed or been directly involved in a traumatic incident is Critical Incident Stress Debriefing, or CISD. These formal psychological debriefing sessions are usually arranged no sooner than forty-eight to seventy-two hours after an event and are designed to help minimise negative psychological effects. They are used more commonly for groups of people rather than for individuals, for example, for staff in banks, building societies, fast food restaurants, etc.

The way a person processes individual psychological reactions to a trauma is rather like the way a technician processes a roll of film: it takes a certain amount of time for the images to develop. Up to seventy-two hours after a traumatic incident, people may still be numbed and in shock and so will not have had sufficient time to process their psychological images of the event. It is simply not possible to debrief someone who is still in a shocked and numbed state. In addition, this length of time also allows for individuals to gain information on what may have happened to loved ones, other members of the group and passers-by.

The number of debriefing sessions arranged can vary. Elizabeth Doggart, co-author of *Understanding Trauma*, is a psychiatric nurse, counsellor and psychotherapist specialising in trauma care and particularly in Critical Incident Stress Debriefing. Most of the people she works with have been directly involved in or have witnessed a violent incident — hold-ups at knife or gunpoint, hostage-taking situations, psychotic episodes, shootings or murder. Others, including care workers, may have had to cope with finding decomposing bodies in houses or flats, for example, or be faced with situations which make a huge visual and sensory impact.

## Group Debriefing

Elizabeth Doggart works mainly for building societies and local authorities all over the UK and says that when she gives a debriefing, it is usually a one-off session lasting about three hours. It is usually carried out with a group rather than a single individual. During the debriefing session, she helps each person review the traumatic incident and the impressions it created for them. The debriefer takes the group through what happened, starting from just prior to the event itself — for example, what he or she was doing at the time and what detail is remembered. One debriefing session is usually sufficient. However, a special follow-up session may be arranged several weeks after the initial debriefing to ascertain how each person has adjusted to daily living in the interim.

It is important to stress that debriefing is not a stand-alone treatment. Its main function is to reassure people that the symptoms they are experiencing are a normal reaction to an abnormal experience and that they are not 'going mad'.

Debriefing and counselling are not the same thing. Debriefing may be followed by specialist counselling sessions, which may continue for weeks or months afterwards, depending on the individual case. For most people, one debriefing session will be sufficient. However, if a person has also been exposed to a number of other stressors, such as those listed on the Holmes and Rahe scale of life events (see page 9), these could negatively influence the overall outcome for the individual concerned. Likewise, a critical incident can have the effect of restimulating a totally unrelated trauma, such as childhood physical, sexual or emotional abuse.

The advantage of group debriefing is that each member of the group gets to hear the story of what happened from the individual perspective of all those involved. Debriefers take each member of the group through a structured set of questions, to encourage individual group members to talk about his or her experiences. This is important for individuals, who may have been held hostage in a separate area; or been ordered to lie flat on the floor throughout an incident; or for people who did not have a full view of what happened. As a result of the group sharing information, everyone gets to understand and appreciate what happened and gains a fuller picture of the event.

During the debriefing sessions, the therapist will also catalogue some of the more common aspects of psychological and physical reactions to trauma. This particular aspect of the process carries certain stress-proofing benefits. People realise that they do not need to feel embarrassed in front of colleagues if symptoms such as flashbacks or feelings of panic or out-of-character behaviour occur, even many months later.

Many organisations make debriefing mandatory, for example, for individuals such as train, tube or bus drivers who have unwittingly been involved in suicide attempts. Drivers may be traumatised by these experiences and torture themselves afterwards with statements such as: 'If only I had put the brakes on a little earlier' and 'should I have seen them coming?'

As well as taking the individual through what happened just before, during and after the incident, debriefers also help individuals to consider the impact of any past life events which may affect the person's ability to deal with the experience.

The main aim of all debriefing sessions is to enable people to integrate the experience into their daily life, to provide perspective and to give an individual more control over what is happening to them. Each person also gains some idea of how long they can expect the whole process to take, and they will be directed to a list of resources and available support services, should they need them at a later date.

## How Effective is CISD?

In recent years, there has been some controversy over the effectiveness of Critical Incident Stress Debriefing. Some research evidence has suggested that CISD may not be effective and, possibly, may cause greater distress to certain sorts of people. However, the research has tended to focus on individual rather than group debriefing, for which CISD was originally devised. As no research into the efficacy of group debriefing exists, and as the research that has been undertaken with individuals is rather small scale, the jury is still out on this aspect.

From the anecdotal evidence gained from individuals who have experienced debriefing and the case files of debriefers, CISD does seem to have positive effects for many people. However, it is crucial that the debriefer is properly trained and supported in his or her work.

People often make the assumption that emergency services personnel such as doctors, nurses, firemen, police officers and search and rescue workers are immune to trauma. While their training equips them to be better stress-proofed than the average person, they can and do experience trauma-related symptoms. For example, firemen often report that even though they risk their lives frequently, it is not the constant risk-taking element of the job that overloads their capacity to deal with trauma. Rather it is certain types of incidents, such as those involving children, which may 'tip them over the edge'.

## Emergency Services Personnel and Trauma

For other groups of emergency services workers, incidents where they feel their skills are inadequate to the task in hand make them particularly vulnerable to the effects of trauma. These types of incidents include: those where equipment does not function properly; the best efforts to resuscitate a victim fail; if a colleague is either killed or seriously injured while on duty; if a colleague commits suicide; or where the emergency service worker accidentally kills or injures someone while on their way to the incident. In addition, incidents involving children or those classified as major disasters, as well as dealing with victims who are family members, friends or colleagues can also cause distress. In any of those instances, the overall sense of powerlessness and distress that can ensue may lead to the development of PTSD.

The change from competent, coping professional to traumatised incapacitated professional can be as instantaneous as it is devastating. In the biblical words used by Dr Jeffrey Mitchell, President of the International Critical Incident Stress Foundation, Associate Professor of Emergency Health Services at the University of Maryland and a leading expert in critical incident stress management: 'in an instant, in the twinkling of an eye, you shall be changed'.

Dr Mitchell describes one case on which he was consulted which graphically illustrates the unpredictable nature of PTSD.

### Mark's Story

Mark was a busy para-medic, who in his fifteen-year career had dealt with between 10,000 and 15,000 call-outs, ranging from fires, floods and tornadoes to road traffic accidents, deaths of babies and nasty cases of child abuse. At no point in his exemplary career had he exhibited any unusual signs of stress. In fact, he had always coped admirably and, by any standards, he would have been regarded as a 'stress hardy' personality type. However, one day he and his partner were called out to assist at a road traffic accident. A woman bled to death in Mark's arms. As a result, both paramedic's clothes were completely drenched with blood. Following the incident, the two men manifested fundamentally different reactions to the event. Mark's partner returned home, showered and changed into fresh clothes. He described the accident scene to his family, and, although upset, his life quickly resumed as normal.

Having cleaned up Mark did not describe the nature of the accident to his family either that day, or subsequently. Although happily married, he could not bring himself to hold or hug either his wife or his two small children. For the next five years, he suffered severe PTSD symptoms, including recurring nightmares. Throughout this period, he continued to be unable to hold or hug his wife and children. As he explained to a trauma counsellor many years later, his fantasy was that if he ever touched them, they too would bleed to death. Although at an intellectual level he knew this was illogical, he still could not manage to override this thought process.

Trauma counselling could have been of help to Mark if he had been offered it soon after the event. However, he did not receive specialist treatment till some five years later. He never thought to seek it and his employers didn't offer it. In the intervening period, he was unable to continue working as a paramedic and was unemployed for three years. It is perhaps a pity that Mark was not offered CISD, as this might have alerted him to the need for specialist help at an earlier stage.

Although unusual, this case is by no means untypical. According to Dr Mitchell, studies carried out in the USA found that while life-time incidence of PTSD among the general population is of the order of two per cent, his research indicates that among emergency services personnel that figure stands at about four per cent and, in certain circumstances, it increases dramatically. For example, if an individual has been a victim of rape or serious sexual assault, the incidence rises to fifty per cent and, if they have been a victim of incest, the figure can be as high as sixty-five per cent.

Not surprisingly, Dr Mitchell's research indicates a direct correlation between the number of critical incidents emergency services personnel are exposed to and their statistical chances of succumbing to PTSD at some stage during their careers. Even for highly trained and stress-hardy individuals, a critical incident stress reaction can quickly become Post-Traumatic Stress Disorder, although not all people exposed to traumatic events go on to develop PTSD. With proper management, a worker's chances of developing PTSD are greatly reduced. With intervention, there is a better than even chance of full recovery. Without it, the disorder can be life-long.

## The Aftermath of Disaster

Dr Mitchell has been consulted on and has directed emergency services crew operations and has provided on-site support for rescue workers and victims of many major incidents — for example, the Oklahoma City Bombing, the TWA Flight 800 crash, the Swiss Air crash in Nova Scotia, the aftermath of Hurricane Hugo in Carolina and Hurricane Andrew in Florida, as well as earthquakes in San Francisco and Los Angeles. Dr Mitchell says that unlike the normal procedures which apply in a non-disaster situation (i.e. providing psychological support as soon as possible after the event), his teams rarely do full psychological debriefings with emergency crews until days, or even weeks, after a disaster. In order to be able to function and focus on the task in hand, crews have no option but to suppress their emotional reactions until after their work has been completed.

**Critical Incident Stress Management (CISM)**
In situations where rescue work is likely to go on for some days, Dr Mitchell advocates giving emergency personnel a short de-briefing session at the end of their first day on-site. This component of Critical Incident Stress Management is called demobilisation. During this session, he advises those present to take a number of stress-proofing precautions — for example, to decrease rather than increase caffeine intake, to avoid or consume alcohol moderately, to be careful about diet and exercise regimes and to get as much rest as possible. Keeping family members as informed and as reassured as possible about issues such as their personal safety and their use of appropriate equipment are also important. Perhaps most importantly of all, he alerts workers to anticipate distressing reactions to the incident afterwards — always emphasising that these are normal reactions to abnormal events.

*Core Components of CISM*

Although the core components of Critical Incident Stress Management were originally developed for emergency services personnel operating in the United States, CISM is inherently flexible and can be modified so to make it equally applicable to any organisation or constituent group.

The core components of CISM are:

○ *Pre-incident education/mental preparedness training*
According to Dr Mitchell, no other CISM component can match education and training for its importance, as it is

always better to teach people about stress as part of their normal training programme than to wait until they encounter a seriously stressful incident

- *Individual crisis intervention support/on-scene support*
  This technique focuses on the needs of single individuals and does not interfere with the overall operations or general staffing issues. It can be provided by specially trained paramedics or by members of their peer group, but is usually given by mental health professionals

- *Demobilisation*
  Used after disasters, prolonged incidents or large-scale events. One of the rarest of all crisis intervention services, it usually comprises a ten-minute informational lecture, followed by twenty minutes of rest and food

- *Critical Incident Stress Debriefing (CISD)*
  Structured group meeting in which a distressing traumatic event is discussed. Designed to mitigate the impact of a traumatic event and accelerate recovery. It is not a stand-alone process and should always be utilised within the context of a complete stress management programme. It is a useful tool for identifying any members of a group who may need additional assistance, such as a referral for psychotherapy

- *Significant support services for families and children*
  Stress is easier to tolerate if emergency workers have a supportive climate around them. Many US organisations offer support services in the form of spouse group debriefings and family crisis counselling, as well as specific critical incident education programmes

○   *Follow up services and professional referrals*
    A comprehensively designed CISM programme makes provision for follow-up to a range of agencies offering support either in the form of psychological, psychiatric or medical services, religious services, family support services or counselling/advice on financial aid, career or legal issues.

## THE BENEFITS OF CISM

According to Dr Mitchell, in an ideal world, companies, organisations and statutory bodies would have all the foregoing elements in place if they were intent on maximising the efficiency of their Critical Incident Stress Management programmes, while minimising the impact of those incidents on individuals. Although most experts agree that the United States has led the field in terms of developing an integrated and multi-component approach to CISM, this model is not being replicated in every country. The false belief that it is expensive to implement a comprehensive programme within the constraints of a public service budget is one argument. Lack of access to information, training and resources is another. Lack of awareness about CISM and fears of increased disability claims, or general disagreement on approach to this strategy, are among the other contra-arguments used.

Dr Mitchell and other researchers can produce impressive statistics to argue the long-term economic benefits of implementing a comprehensive CISM programme — for example, reduced incidence of sick leave, faster return to normal life functions and worker productivity, smaller medical compensation claims and reduced legal expenses. Public service authorities outside the United States are slow to rise to the challenge. Conversely, certain areas of the private sector, including rail companies, airlines and the oil industry are more responsive to this concept. However, this may have more to do with mitigating their loss in the event of litigation than any other overriding consideration.

While cost may be an issue in designing an effective CISM programme, not all elements of the programme are cost-intensive. For example, one of the approaches Dr Mitchell favours is using peer group support personnel to supplement the services being provided by mental health professionals, as this achieves maximum effect for minimum expenditure.

Typically, a Critical Incident Stress Management team comprises a mix of fire fighters, nurses, doctors, paramedics, police officers, life guards, prison officers or chaplains and safety officials, as well as psychiatrists, psychologists and social workers. With highly specialised training of no more than six days duration, group critical incident support techniques can be extremely effective. Group interaction removes the fallacy of uniqueness and reinforces the message that people are experiencing normal reactions to abnormal events. The stress management techniques they offer are never confused with therapy. In fact, these 'extenders' are specifically trained not to exceed the limits of their training and to recognise when it is essential to make referrals to properly qualified health professionals.

## CHAPTER 13

# How to Choose a Therapist

Many people do not understand what counselling and psychotherapy involve or how to choose an appropriate therapist. The British Association for Counselling describe the nature of counselling in their Code of Ethics and Practice for Counsellors as:

> The overall aim of counselling is to provide an opportunity for the client to work towards living in a way that he or she experiences as more satisfying and resourceful... Counselling may be concerned with developmental issues, addressing and resolving specific problems, making decisions, coping with crises, developing personal insight and knowledge, working through feelings of inner conflict or improving relationships with others. The counsellor's role is to facilitate the client's work in ways which respect the client's values, personal resources and capacity for choice within his or her cultural context.

The Association also goes on to state that:

> There is no generally accepted distinction between counselling and psychotherapy. There are well-founded traditions which use the terms interchangeably and others which distinguish between them.

Counsellors and psychotherapists do not, unless medically qualified, prescribe any type of medication. Counsellors and psychotherapists work with a variety of clients and client problems — for example, young people in youth centres and specialist counselling services, or in schools as school counsellors. Some counsellors are employed to work in medical settings, such as doctors' surgeries and counselling services run by hospitals. Others work in the private sector as workplace counsellors and some are self-employed and work in private practice.

## Professional Associations

The United Kingdom Council for Psychotherapy (UKCP) offers a UK-based register of psychotherapists. The UKCP represents a number of theoretical schools and each school has its own branch. Individuals have to belong to a specialist training organisation or professional body representing one of the theoretical schools and demonstrate a baseline training and competency within that theoretical school to become eligible for registration. Acceptance on to the UKCP register allows the individual to use the words, 'UKCP Registered', after his or her name. The type of training undertaken by the individual is also stated in each case, for example UKCP Registered Cognitive-Behavioural Psychotherapist. There are currently five branches within the UKCP: Psychoanalytic, Humanistic and Integrative, Family, Contructivist and Cognitive-Behavioural.

The British Association for Counselling also has a scheme to recognise the competence of counsellors, called accreditation. To become eligible for accreditation, a counsellor has to have completed a minimum of 450 hours of basic training, have practical experience of a minimum of 450 client hours and meet a range of other professional requirements. The individual's application is then vetted and, if successful, the applicant can then use the words BAC Registered Practitioner after his or her name. Accredited counsellors have to reapply for accreditation every five years.

In addition, a new counsellor register has been set up in the UK called the United Kingdom Register of Counsellors. Counsellors must already either be individually accredited or work for an agency such as RELATE or CRUSE as a trained volunteer counsellor. There are currently two routes on to the register. One is the individual accredited counsellor, who may use the words UKRC Registered Independent Counsellor or Reg. Ind. Couns. The second route, for those who are sponsored as a volunteer counsellor, is Registered Sponsored Counsellor. However, such counsellors are not allowed to use this title after their name. The sponsoring organisation, such as RELATE or CRUSE, is allowed to use the UKRC logo on letterhead and promotional material. Once a counsellor has ceased to be a volunteer with the sponsored organisation, he or she loses the right to be called a Registered Sponsored Counsellor.

The British Psychological Society (BPS) also has its own recognition scheme, which is called chartership. A psychologist with additional specialist training in counselling can apply to become what is known as a Chartered Counselling Psychologist. There are also specialist professional bodies, such as the British Association for Behavioural and Cognitive Psychotherapies (BABCP), who also accredit psychotherapists. You may see the words BABCP Accredited Cognitive-

Behavioural Psychotherapist after the name of someone accredited with such a body. Most of these bodies also belong to UKCP.

Accreditation, registration and chartership minimise the chances of receiving poor counselling or psychotherapy. However, it is important to remember that therapists are human beings. Human beings are fallible and make mistakes, and counselling or psychotherapy may not always be the most appropriate form of help for an individual's problem. For example, a woman on a top floor flat with two small children living on benefits with little social support may find it helpful in a supportive way to talk to a counsellor. However, her main problems may be social isolation, lack of money and poor accommodation and she may be better off talking to an advice worker who may be able to offer practical advice and support. Sadly, some people come into counselling believing that the counsellor has a 'magic wand' to make everything right. Even if counselling can help with an individual's problem, some people seem surprised that they may have to take responsibility for practising agreed exercises or homework assignments. Always trust your own judgment about any professional person you come into contact with, and check whether your counsellor or psychotherapist is receiving clinical supervision (a professional requirement, and one which also acts as a type of 'quality control'). Ask your counsellor or psychotherapist to explain how he or she believes their particular type of therapy (currently there are 440 known therapies) will help you. If you are at all unsure or uncomfortable, then make the decision to find another person to work with you.

## What is a Good Therapist?

A good therapist is likely to offer an explanation of what is causing your problems at a pace and in a way you will understand. The person should also be able to give you some sense of how long you will be in therapy and the kind of process it will involve. The style of interaction of the therapist will reflect the theoretical school he or she belongs to. For example, some counsellors will be highly active and you will be asked to undertake assignments, write things down and complete exercises. Other will say very little and expect you to do all the talking.

It is perfectly acceptable to shop around to find the right person to help you. A personal recommendation from a doctor or close friend is probably the easiest way to get the selection process moving. Professional bodies such as the British Association for Counselling, UKCP, UKRC, BABCP and BPS keep a list of accredited counsellors (see pages 197 and 204 for contact details).

### Checklist to Use

The following checklist was developed by Dr Stephen Palmer and Kasia Szymanska, at the Centre for Stress Management, London:

- ○ check that your counsellor has relevant qualifications and experience in the field of counselling/psychotherapy
- ○ ask about the type of approach the counsellor uses and how it relates to your problem
- ○ ask if the counsellor is in clinical counselling supervision. (Most professional bodies consider supervision to be mandatory)

- ask if the counsellor, or counselling agency, is a member of a professional body and abides by the code of ethics. If possible, obtain a copy of the code
- discuss your goals and expectations
- ask about your counsellor's fee structure, if appropriate, and, if you are on a low income, check if the counsellor operates on a sliding scale. Discuss the frequency and estimated duration of the counselling
- arrange regular review sessions with your counsellor to evaluate your progress
- do not enter into a long-term counselling contract unless you are satisfied that it is necessary and beneficial to you.

If you do not have a chance to discuss the above points during your first session, do so at the next possible opportunity.

In addition to the above, Palmer and Szymanska also discuss a number of other points that you should keep in mind when working with a counsellor. These are:

- that counsellor self-disclosure can sometimes be therapeutically useful. However, if the sessions are dominated by the counsellor discussing his or her own problems at length, this may not be appropriate and you should raise this issue in the counselling session. If at any time you feel discounted, undermined or manipulated within the session, discuss this with the counsellor too. It is easier to resolve issues as and when they arise

- you should not accept significant gifts from your counsellor. This does not apply to relevant therapeutic material. Neither should you accept social invitations from your counsellor, for example, dining in a restaurant or going for a drink. However, this does not apply to relevant therapeutic assignments, such as being accompanied by your counsellor into a situation to help you overcome a phobia

- if your counsellor proposes a change in venue for the counselling sessions without good reason, do not agree, for example, on a move from a centre to the counsellor's own home unless you are totally satisfied with the reason for the move

- research has shown that it is not beneficial for clients to have sexual contact with their counsellor. Professional counselling and psychotherapy bodies consider it unethical for counsellors or therapists to engage in a sexual relationship with current clients.

If you have any doubts about the counselling you are receiving, then discuss them with your counsellor. If you are still uncertain, seek advice — perhaps from a friend, your doctor, your local Citizens Advice Bureau, the professional body your counsellor belongs to or the counselling agency that may employ your counsellor. If you are still unsure that you and the therapist are the right fit, a sensible guideline is to commit to no more than two or three sessions to establish whether this is a person with whom you are comfortable. Remember that you have the right to terminate counselling whenever you choose.

## POST-TRAUMATIC STRESS COUNSELLING

Most European countries claim to have a number of post-traumatic stress counsellors, but, unfortunately, the ranges and standards of training are not uniform throughout. Many psychiatrists claim to be able to treat PTSD, yet the profession's general training programme does not specifically cover this area. Some chartered psychologists/clinical psychologists have special training in this area, others do not. Anyone seeking professional help should check a counsellor's qualifications, training, clinical experience and other credentials carefully.

According to Roger Le Duc-Barnett, a consultant supervisor at the Trauma Support Centre at Beckenham in Kent and ex-Chair of the British Association for Counselling's Trauma Care Committee, choosing the right trauma counsellor can be quite confusing. At the time of writing, professional qualifications are not standardised (although by the time this book is published, that may have changed). To further complicate the picture, the number of appropriately qualified therapists in Britain is still quite small.

Roger Le Duc-Barnett recommends that before making a final choice, a client should:

- attend an initial interview or talk on the telephone with the proposed therapist and ascertain his or her previous training and experience in the trauma field

- ask which therapeutic model the trauma therapist uses — for example, Cognitive-Behavioural, Psychodynamic, or Person-Centred, and how the therapist sees their approach being of help to you and your trauma-related problem
- if the trauma victim knows another therapist, ask for a professional opinion of the proposed trauma counsellor.

**Cognitive Behavioural Model**

Of all the various counselling therapies available, Roger Le Duc-Barnett favours the cognitive-behavioural model. One of the main reasons for choosing this model is that people who have been traumatised do not need to spend several months trying to reduce their symptoms. Resolution can, in fact, be achieved very quickly. Secondly, a more actively focused and structured therapy reduces the client's personal feelings of chaos, confusion and anxiety.

Research has shown that cognitive-behavioural counselling is both effective and efficient in dealing with a range of psychological problems. Problems such as anxiety, depression, stress and obsessional compulsive disorder are areas in which cognitive-behavioural counselling excel. As cognitive-behavioural counselling is more collaborative in style, the client is enlisted in practical ways of helping him or herself.

CHAPTER 14

# New Treatments

## EMDR

At the time of writing, EMDR (Eye Movement Desensitisation and Reprocessing) is one of the newer therapies being used for treating people who are re-experiencing the vivid images generated by traumatic incidents such as road traffic accidents, rail crashes, shootings or disasters.

Researchers have not arrived at a consensus about how EMDR works, although there are many theories about the possible ways it affects the processing of information between the left and the right sides of the brain. In normal circumstances, the brain processes information in a series of logical sequences, rather like the way a computer creates and stores documents and files. However, in a traumatic incident, where events happen extremely rapidly (especially incidents such as car accidents or shootings), the brain may be bombarded with visual, auditory and sensory images faster than it can process and store them. Rather like a circuit board in the process of going haywire, instead of 'storing neat files of data', everything may end up swimming around in the brain in a state of total confusion.

The underlying principle of EMDR is to restore some order and logic to that visual, auditory and sensory confusion, by recalling the images in a very controlled fashion. The process is simplicity itself. It involves making the patient describe the incident in graphic detail, recalling it virtually frame by frame, almost as if the person was rewinding a video tape slowly. Throughout the description he or she is asked to keep his or her eyes open and follow the therapist's finger-waving or hand-tapping movements simultaneously. The procedure is brief and it is focused. It is rather like the technique used by hypnotists, but all comparisons with hypnotism end here. Sessions are always one-to-one and tend to last for about forty-five minutes each. It can take as little as one or as many as five sessions before a patient feels an improvement.

Experts agree that EMDR should only be carried out by skilled therapists. If it is not done expertly, a patient runs the risk of being caused further psychological damage. Patients often become extremely upset during these image-recalling sessions. As well as being tearful, they may also experience breathing difficulties and their heart rate can increase dramatically. It is essential, therefore, that the person practising this therapy possesses the requisite skills and training for dealing with those reactions.

EMDR was originally developed by Dr Francine Shapiro, an independent psychologist working in the US. While it is still the subject of some controversy, many psychiatrists and mental health professionals have been encouraged by the results it has achieved for their patients. Dr Jeffrey Mitchell, President of the International Critical Incident Stress Foundation and Associate Professor of Emergency Health Services at the University of Maryland, is an enthusiastic supporter of EMDR. He describes it as one of the best tools he has used for helping both emergency services personnel and private citizens who have been involved in disasters.

That said, Dr Mitchell stresses that not everybody is a suitable candidate for this therapy. In fact, he always chooses potential candidates extremely carefully. For example, he does not advocate using it in cases where the patient is having 'out of body' experiences, is suffering from serious disassociative disorders or is abusing alcohol or other mind-altering drugs. In short, if the trauma reaction is complicated by pre-existing psychological or psychiatric problems, then Dr Mitchell would not favour using it. Likewise, if the patient does not have an adequate family or social support structure, he would tend to err on the side of caution. For example, he would never allow a patient to return to an empty home after a session. Other aspects of candidate selection are also extremely important. Dr Mitchell believes it works best in cases where the patient is suffering extreme distress as a result of experiencing recurring visual images of the critical incident.

Dr Mitchell describes one woman he treated who had been involved in an attempted car-jacking by armed men at a motorway intersection near Pittsburgh, Pennsylvania. As soon as she realised what was happening, she almost froze with terror, as she had read newspaper reports of several other car-jackings in that district. In three of those instances, the car-jackers had fired gun shots. This woman, however, was lucky in two respects. Firstly, she had activated the central locking system when she had started her journey, and so the gunmen were unable to open any of the car doors. Secondly, she reacted extremely quickly by stepping on the accelerator and taking off at high speed, narrowly missing being hit by oncoming traffic.

For several days afterwards, she experienced classic PTSD symptoms and she could neither sleep nor work. Any reference to the incident caused her to burst into tears. However, within thirty minutes of starting her first EMDR session, she was greatly improved. The rest of her therapy comprised a series of homework assignments where Dr Mitchell asked her to return to the incident site, firstly with her husband and later on her own. After twenty-four hours, she was well enough to return to work and the horrendous nightmares she had been suffering from had receded, although they did not disappear entirely for another two weeks.

## Learning about Trauma

In medical and psychological treatment terms trauma is still a relatively new concept and practitioners are learning more all the time about how people become traumatised and what interventions aid recovery. Ten years ago in the United Kingdom, a range of techniques which were met with scepticism have now become standard psychological interventions. This is both an exciting and humbling field of human endeavour to be involved in: exciting because knowledge grows almost daily; and humbling because as more becomes known, the more practitioners realise there is to know.

CHAPTER 15

# More Ways to Help Yourself: Overcoming Depression, Guilt, Anger and Anxiety

> HEALTH WARNING
>
> *This section of the book offers a variety of techniques which many people have found useful. Although of great value, they should not be seen as a substitute for professional advice and support. If in doubt, talk to your doctor or make contact with a professional body such as the British Association for Counselling (see page 197). You may also find it useful to seek information and advice from one of the specialist organisations listed on pages 194–205.*

There are numerous techniques that can help a person deal with difficult emotions and situations. It is impossible to offer them all in one chapter. Therefore, this chapter will focus on a limited range of self-help techniques you can engage in. Further Reading provides details of a number of publications, many of which provide an excellent range of useful and practical techniques that can be safely carried out by the reader.

## DEPRESSION

There are many times in life when we feel low and dispirited and on these occasions we may use the word depressed to describe how we are feeling. However, depression is more than a simple sense of feeling low and is treated as an illness (outlined in *DSM IV* — the major diagnostic tool used) by the medical profession. Feeling low in mood is something which usually lasts only a brief period of time, whereas depression is likely to worsen over time.

Depression can be triggered by a physical problem, such as an underactive thyroid or through alcohol or drug misuse. Some people may be genetically predisposed towards depression, as there is evidence that depression can run in families. However, it may take a life event to act as the trigger for the depression. There is now some evidence to demonstrate a link between depression and exposure to stress.

Some people find they become depressed slowly over a period of time and they may not even realise they are depressed. Energy levels drop, work performance deteriorates, the person loses the ability to communicate with those around them and he or she experiences a decrease in quality of life. Many people who experience sleeping problems, aches or pains of unknown origin, weight loss/gain, stomach problems and extreme tiredness can be suffering from depression without realising it. Over ten years ago the Mental Health Foundation produced a report based on research which had been undertaken by two general practitioners. This suggested that approximately two-thirds of people attending GP surgeries with physical symptoms were, in fact, depressed.

Recognising the problem and getting help is the key to getting depression under control. You can then seek psychotherapy or counselling, or take some other course of personal action. The checklist that follows may be the first step in that process.

## Depression Checklist

If you answer *'YES' to 5 or more of the following* it may indicate that you are depressed and it would be helpful for you to make an appointment to see your doctor.

| *Symptom* | Yes | No |
|---|---|---|
| Feeling empty or sad, perhaps tearful | | |
| Loss of interest or pleasure in daily activities | | |
| Weight loss when not dieting | | |
| Difficulty sleeping | | |
| Restlessness, muscle twitching | | |
| Tiredness and/or loss of energy | | |
| Loss of self-esteem, feelings of worthlessness | | |
| Unable to concentrate or make decisions | | |
| Thoughts of death, perhaps thoughts of suicide | | |

As already mentioned, although some people may have a genetic predisposition towards depression, it is more likely that it is their thinking style that is making them depressed. For example, there is some research which indicates a difference between the thinking styles and associated outcomes for optimists and pessimists. Optimists are more likely to have happier lives, more fulfilling relationships, live longer and heal more quickly than pessimists. The only difference between an optimist and a pessimist is that optimists try to make the best of the situation they find themselves in, while minimising negative thinking wherever possible. Depressed people tend to think in a negative way. As mentioned in Chapter 6, Our Assumptions About the World, people can have a negative view of themselves 'I'm useless', of others 'No-one understands', and of the world 'Life has no meaning'. Negative thinking styles make depression worse, as these thoughts tend to stop people from dealing with problems.

### Activity Scheduling

Depression slows you down physically and mentally, and you may feel that everyday activities are more of an effort. Those people who engage in activity tend to recover more quickly. It is therefore important for people who are depressed to engage as fully as possible in the world around them, even though this is usually the last thing they feel like doing. For this reason, it is a good idea to design an activity schedule of the things you intend to do. Such as:

| Time | Sunday | Monday | Tuesday | Wednesday | Thursday | Friday | Saturday |
|---|---|---|---|---|---|---|---|
| 8–9 | Breakfast | Breakfast | | | | | |
| 9–10 | Ring Mike | Ring Mum | | | | | |
| 10–11 | Go to park for a walk | Go to supermarket | | | | | |
| 11–12 | Clean kitchen | Have coffee and read paper in local cafe | | | | | |
| 12–1 | Lunch | Look round shops | | | | | |
| 1–2 | Clear up lunch dishes | Lunch | | | | | |
| 2–3 | Read a book | Watch TV | | | | | |
| 4–5 | Ring Jane | See Sue | | | | | |
| 5–6 | Use Internet | | | | | | |

| Time | Sunday | Monday | Tuesday | Wednesday | Thursday | Friday | Saturday |
|---|---|---|---|---|---|---|---|
| 6–7 | Prepare Tuesday's activity schedule | | | | | | |
| 7–8 | Dinner | Dinner with Sue | | | | | |
| 8–9 | Watch TV | Prepare Wednesday's activity schedule | | | | | |
| 9–10 | Read in bed | Read in bed | | | | | |
| 10–11 | Sleep | Sleep | | | | | |

Activity helps you feel less tired, encourages you to do more and to think more clearly. You will find that at the beginning you will need to take one hour at a time. Many people find that committing a list of tasks to paper makes carrying out those tasks less difficult, providing a sense of control over what is happening and pride at what has been achieved. It is important to try and get a balance between activities which might be stretching and activities which are easy to cope with. When people are depressed, they may isolate themselves from activities that they previously enjoyed. For example, having a massage or a sauna, going window shopping, having a coffee and watching the world go by from a local coffee bar, having a facial or some other beauty treatment, etc. It is important that your activity schedule also includes some of these activities. Although you may feel that you will not enjoy them as much as you used to do, you may also find that they raise your spirits more than you thought they would.

These activities are particularly relevant for people who 'blame' themselves for feeling the way they do. These are the people who give themselves no credit for anything they achieve, who therefore believe they 'should' be using the time off work to clean the house or decorate the kitchen, rather than allowing time to pamper themselves as well as undertake chores.

It can also be helpful to make a list of all the items you have put off and then rate each of those items in terms of perceived difficulty, for example by using a scale of 0–8:

0 1 2 3 4 5 6 7 8
(0 = no difficulty and 8 = a high degree of difficulty)

| | | |
|---|---|---|
| a walk in the park | = | 3 (little difficulty) |
| ring Jane | = | 2 (very little difficulty) |
| clean kitchen | = | 7 (very difficult because it's in a huge mess!) |

Once you have drawn up this list, choose items which have a rating between 3 and 5. Anything rated higher than 5 may be too difficult for you at the beginning of the process. Conversely, anything less than a 3 may be too easy. On the other hand, a rating of 3 or less could indicate some form of pleasant activity to fill in the time which doesn't use too much effort. Always remember to congratulate yourself on your achievements: reflect on *what you have* managed to do rather than on what you believe you *should* have been doing. Keeping a record like this provides you with evidence of what you have achieved. Everyone has bad days when it is easy to feel that nothing has been achieved. A written record of the improvements you have made can help to provide a realistic balance of progress for just such days.

### Medication

It is important to consider the role, if any, of medication. In the last few years antidepressants have become widely used. Antidepressants were discovered in the 1950s and research into their effectiveness has meant that the 1990s now see a range of sophisticated medication available to those who suffer from depression. Antidepressants tend to be recommended for moderate to severe levels of depression, although they can and have been used in milder cases. Some medications are initially taken at a low dosage and built up over time, while some of the newer drugs have a standard dosage and positive effects are not seen for two weeks or more. It is important to understand that the drug needs time to take effect and results are not immediate. Once the person's symptoms have reduced, usually over a six-to eight-week period, a further four to six months treatment is recommended to ensure a positive outcome. Following this period, the medication is usually reduced rather than abruptly stopped.

Many people do not like taking medication for fear that they will become dependent on it. However, there is no evidence that the newer drugs cause any type of dependency, and withdrawal from medication too soon may lead to relapse. Antidepressants work by altering the chemical make-up of the brain. Depression tends to alter the way the brain operates and antidepressant drugs work on correcting this alteration.

As with any prescribed drug, it is important that you inform your GP of your progress, as he or she may be able to alter the dosage or type of drug given. Your doctor will also be happy to discuss any side-effects, such as a dry mouth, sleepiness etc., so that you are fully briefed on any symptoms you may experience.

Some people have chosen alternative medicine such as St John's Wort — a plant recognised to have antidepressant characteristics and which is prescribed by doctors quite freely in countries such as Germany. St John's Wort is freely available as an over-the-counter purchase from health food shops. However, although many people have found this product of help, recent research has indicated that St John's Wort can interfere with the effects of some forms of medication and it would be advisable to consult with your GP before taking any substance. It is also unlikely that St John's Wort would be able to provide an effective treatment for those suffering from severe depression.

Developing a healthy thinking style is also crucial to minimising or eradicating depressive feelings. See Chapter 6, Our Assumptions About the World: How Thinking Style Helps or Hinders, to remind you about how to change your self-defeating thoughts.

# Guilt

Guilt may be regarded as an unhelpful emotion. Professor Windy Dryden, a psychologist, lecturer and writer, believes that for guilt to exist, three conditions are required:

1. You must believe that you have gone against a value or principle that you adhere to and you also have to see things in absolutist terms. For example: 'I must never ever put myself before others, or consider myself above others.'

2. You focus on the consequences of what you have done or should not have done, as the case may be. For example: 'I shouldn't have been speeding in the first place', 'I should have warned that woman.'

3. You hold an unshakeable belief that, somehow, you are guilty, merely by existing in this world. Someone who feels guilty, but cannot tell you why, typifies this kind of guilt.

The first two types of guilt are about *actions we have taken*, or *choices we have made*, and the consequences of those choices. The third type of guilt is something Professor Dryden describes as 'existential guilt'. It stays with the person throughout life, unless they change the way they view the world. Sometimes good people do bad things and we may regret our actions.

### Survivor Guilt

Survivor guilt has a particular resonance within the context of this book. As its name suggests, survivors may suffer great distress as a result of being rescued from a critical incident or a disaster in which other people were unlucky enough to die. The person will be dominated by thoughts such as 'What if?', 'If only', or 'Supposing I had . . .'. Survivors may also dwell endlessly on facts about the critical incident, which only came to light long afterwards. Armed with that information, they may agonise relentlessly about why they did not behave differently at the time. If the sufferer of survivor guilt was also unlucky enough to experience 'existential guilt' before their traumatic event, the guilt that ensues may become too much to bear.

Overall, guilt is an unhelpful emotion. It does not make anything better, whereas other emotions such as regret and remorse may convert into more positive action. If you've made a mistake, then it makes sense to want to put it right. People who feel remorse and regret are more likely to try and do something to put the situation right. On the other hand, those who feel guilty about something are likely to avoid people, places and activities that remind them of the guilt they feel. Alternatively, they may wallow in self-loathing and withdraw from social contact. Such people may subsequently descend into a depressive state.

### Tips for Dealing with Guilt

o Ask yourself what you really feel guilty about.

o Ask yourself if you were to find yourself in exactly the same situation today whether you would behave any differently.

o Identify the core beliefs that influence the way you live your life. Ask yourself whether it is possible for a human being to live up to all of those core beliefs all of the time.

o Remember the maxim set out earlier in this book: 'Bad things happen to good people and good people sometimes do bad things.'

- Examine your 'thinking style' for examples of the kind of self-defeating thoughts described on page 69.
- Learn to accept that you are a fallible human being.
- If there is something you can do to help to ease matters for others, then do so.
- Don't hide away from the world, as this only leads to depression.
- Learn to forgive yourself and remember that forgiveness is a choice that you can choose to exercise on yourself.

You may find it useful to draw a circle and then divide it up, rather like cutting a cake, making each slice of the cake represent how much responsibility you attribute to all those involved in an incident.

*The Responsibility Pie*

- Driver One who moved lanes without indicating
- Me for driving too fast
- Driver Two who was not wearing a seatbelt
- The garage for not checking the brakes on the car correctly

## Big I, Little I

When you find yourself putting yourself down, you can use what is called the 'Big I, Little I' as a way of helping yourself to gain a balanced view of you as a human being.

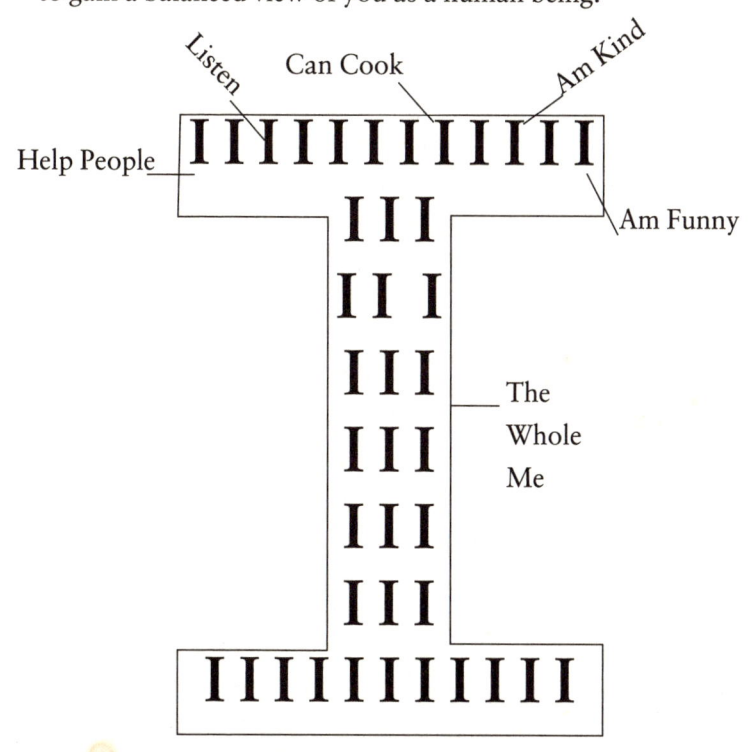

*Listen* — *Can Cook* — *Am Kind*

Help People — [Big I filled with Little Is] — Am Funny

The Whole Me

The 'Big I' represents the whole of you. When you find yourself saying 'Because I did or did not do something, that makes me a bad person,' you are stating in global terms that the whole of the 'Big I' (*you*) is bad. However, if you look inside the figure of the 'Big I', you will see lots of 'Little Is'. These 'Little Is' represent all the parts of yourself which make up the 'Big I'. As you look at all those 'Little Is', make a list of what each of them represents.

For example:

- ○ I am kind to animals
- ○ I help other people
- ○ I have a good sense of humour.

In carrying out this exercise, you will see that although you have made a mistake, the mistake is only one part of you the total person. Using this technique can help you keep life in perspective. Perspective is one of the first things to become distorted when a person is under pressure.

### Cost Benefit Analysis

It can be hard to change your behaviour, particularly if you have been acting in a particular way for months, years or decades. You may not even be certain that you really want to change your behaviour, because behaving in a certain way may be bringing certain pay-offs. A 'cost benefit analysis' can help you understand the benefits a particular behaviour is creating in your life currently.

| Problem: Not Making Decisions | Date: 23.12.2000 |
|---|---|
| *Benefits* | *Costs* |
| 1. Am never wrong | I never learn anything |
| 2. Stops arguments at home | A stagnant relationship which does not develop or grow |

| | |
|---|---|
| 3. Makes me feel safe | False sense of security as my life could change at any time. Never doing the things I would like to. |

When you have written out all the benefits and costs of your behaviour, you will be in a better position to make decisions about whether you wish to remain the same, or wish to change.

## Anger

A healthy emotion is one that is appropriate to the situation and passes without causing damage either to the person concerned or to the people around them. An anger reaction may, indeed, be linked to the 'fight or flight' response referred to in Chapter 1, Understanding Trauma and Stress. Anger has a self-protective role to play in our well-being. No-one would suggest that you should try to suppress this natural reaction totally. It could save your life.

Yet, there is a world of difference between healthy and unhealthy anger. Unhealthy anger is where the anger lingers, festers and is destructive to the individual or to those around them. It can easily turn into rage or violent behaviour to oneself or others. Some research studies suggest there is a strong link between excessive anger and coronary heart disease. Indeed, anger can raise cholesterol levels, aggravate digestive problems, contribute to hypertension and increase sensitivity to pain.

### Your Anger Checklist

If you answer *'Yes'* to any of the following, you are probably experiencing unhealthy anger and would benefit from seeking professional help.

| Symptom | Yes | No |
| --- | --- | --- |
| Feeling angry for no reason | | |
| Taking your feelings out on other people | | |
| Daydreaming about revenge | | |
| Experiencing nightmares about revenge | | |
| Wanting to hit inanimate objects | | |
| Other people have commented on your anger | | |
| Tension, grinding your teeth or clenching your jaw | | |

The chances of feeling anger are likely to be increased if we feel that we (or people we loved) were not treated well, or that we were let down by an organisation (e.g. the emergency services or our employer). In many instances, these feelings of anger will simply subside in time. However, for some people they may continue or even increase in intensity. However, as with any other severe personality change, a visit to a doctor would be well advised.

### Tips for Dealing with Anger

The following is a list of coping strategies, which can be employed if you are unhappy about your anger and wish to gain control of your feelings:

- employ the cognitive skills outlined above. For example, if your thinking contains too many *shoulds* and *musts* about how people behaved, ask yourself if thinking in that way really helps you

- walk away. If you find it really hard to control your anger, then begin by walking away from the situation and taking time to calm down

- use the relaxation techniques outlined later in this chapter on pages 182–5. You may find the breathing exercise the most helpful of all

- learn to be more assertive because assertion skills will provide you with an appropriate way to express verbally what exactly you feel

- avoid alcohol, because this may exaggerate your feelings even more

- avoid drugs (unless prescribed by your doctor). Certain drugs, such as amphetamines, and illegal substances, such as cocaine, will make you feel more angry. Remember that alcohol is also a drug which is a depressant, and can affect your mood and your ability to recover

- plan in advance for any situations which you expect are going to be difficult to manage.

You may also find it useful to keep an anger diary in which you record details of when you become angry, the trigger for your anger, how much anger you feel (using the 0= no anger to 8 = rageful scale), what thoughts were going through your mind at the time and the behaviours you engaged in. Keeping a diary which you make entries into at least once a day for three weeks or more can help you see whether there are patterns to your feelings and behaviours, and what type of situations are likely to trigger your anger. The diary also gives you an opportunity of monitoring how well you are managing your anger, as you can look back to see what has been happening.

## Assertiveness

Assertive people are prepared to ask for what they want and they try not to infringe the rights of others in the process. They look for what is called a 'win-win' scenario. They take responsibility for their own actions and recognise that they have choices, even if those choices are between the lesser of two evils. Becoming more assertive can improve the way we communicate with others. It can minimise unwelcome behaviour (such as aggression) and it can help us feel better about ourselves. Most colleges and evening institutes are likely to offer short courses on assertiveness.

## Shame

Shame manifests itself in many different ways and under many guises. People who feel shame often believe they have fallen short of an ideal — either one that they hold themselves or one that they think others hold. Alternatively, they may feel shame because they know they have behaved in a manner that is frowned upon by society generally, or by specific individuals. This may be so because they are having thoughts for which other people would judge them harshly, because they are experiencing emotions considered unkind or wrong, or because they simply 'don't look right'.

In cognitive terms, this is called 'awfulising' situations.

Examples of awfulising include telling yourself that some aspect of your personality or lifestyle is inadequate or shameful. Very often, awfulising is expressed in terms of criticism about personal weakness: 'If they saw me cry, that would be awful. What would they think of me?'

People who experience shame have a great capacity for avoiding situations, people and places which they believe reminds them of their weakness. They can withdraw in a number of ways. For example, avoiding eye contact is one form of withdrawal. Avoiding social contact is another. Another common expression of shame is to take the view that 'the best form of defence is attack'. People who adopt this stance act out their shame in attacking behaviour. The third and final category of reactive behaviour is abuse of alcohol or drugs — all designed to deaden feelings of shame.

In cognitive psychology, dealing with shame means challenging the way you see yourself and the event that you believe is shameful. (See Negative Thinking Styles, page 69).

## Humiliation

Feeling humiliated is synonymous with believing you have lost status in some way. People who feel humiliated also experience a strong desire for revenge. They tend to believe that if they could inflict damage on the person they hold responsible for their humiliation, they would somehow feel better. Humiliation may be closely linked with the same kind of thought processes aroused by shame and guilt — particularly around the issue of worrying that others would think less of them as a result of their lost status.

Feelings of shame and humiliation often follow experiences such as unwanted sexual encounters, rape and sexual abuse. Not only do the victims feel violated, they also feel tainted and they may believe that others will think less of them as a result. Rape victims, for example, will worry about people thinking they did not fight off their attacker hard enough. Or they may believe people will say they 'asked for what happened', because they behaved in a particular way or took certain kinds of risks.

**Tips for Dealing with Shame and Humiliation**
- Ask yourself if you believe someone thinks less of you as a result of this incident and why.

- Ask yourself if *you* would think less of someone who had gone through an identical experience to your own.

- If your answer to both questions is 'no', then ask yourself why you should hold yourself responsible for the situation in the first place.

## ANXIETY

### How to Worry Constructively

About thirty-nine per cent of the things you worry about never actually come to pass. An additional thirty-two per cent of things you worry about have already happened. A further twenty-one per cent of your worries are over insignificant trivialities. That leaves nine per cent for important matters where you have legitimate cause for concern.

If you stopped worrying completely, you would be of little value to yourself, your employer or your family. A certain amount of worry and tension makes you feel better, so keep on worrying. Concentrate on that nine per cent and put the other ninety-one per cent behind you.

### Keeping a Worry Notebook

A worry notebook will help you worry constructively. Take any notebook and divide it into four sections, using the following headings:

### Things Which Might Happen

1. Worries for today, i.e. things which might possibly happen
2. Worries for today, i.e. things which have already happened

### Today's Real Events

3. Worries for today, i.e. minor, insignificant things
4. Worries for today, i.e. important problems

Make the entries for headings 1, 2 and 3 before you go to bed. Choose the time of day you are at your strongest and brightest to complete section 4.

Section 4 merits special comment. *Worrying about a problem does not solve it, but doing something about it certainly does.* Many people are fearful of making a decision in case it is the wrong one. However, what people forget is that making no decision is decision-making by default. After all, if you take no action, *something will still happen* and only you can decide whether you want to be in control (as much as is possible), or just let the situation happen. There is *always* a choice, even if the choice is between the lesser of two evils.

### Relaxation

When you are feeling anxious, angry or tense it can be useful to do some relaxation exercises. There are many forms of relaxation, ranging from those that require physical exertion or movement, to those that require nothing more than breathing or visualisation techniques. Listed below are four common techniques.

#### *Breathing*

- Breathe in through your nose for a count of 4
- Breathe out through your mouth for a count of 5
- As you breathe out, consciously relax your shoulders

When you breathe in and out, use your stomach muscles to control your breathing. For example, when breathing in, use your stomach muscle to push out; when you breathe out use your stomach muscle to push in. This way you will breathe more deeply, which will help you gain the maximum benefit from this kind of relaxation.

When people are anxious, they tend to breathe shallowly. When this happens, the body gets less oxygen and many people are therefore tempted to breathe faster to make up for this deficit. However, breathing too fast can make a person feel dizzy or faint and may be frightening. This type of breathing can lead to a condition called Hyperventilation, which is described more fully on page 187.

Keep practising the above until you feel confident that you would be able to undertake this breathing exercise anywhere and at any time. It is simple but effective and can take the edge off feelings of nervousness. It is particularly helpful for times when you are about to face a difficult situation, or a confrontation.

## Muscle Tensing Exercise

1. Lie on the floor and make yourself comfortable.

2. Starting with your feet, tense all your muscles and then relax them. Focus on how heavy your feet feel and the way in which they are sinking into the floor.

3. Tense all the muscles in your legs as hard as you possibly can, then relax them. Focus on how heavy your legs feel and the way in which they are sinking into the floor.

4. Move up along through the other parts of your body — hips, stomach, chest, arms, neck and face — tensing and relaxing the muscles as you go.

**Note:** If you suffer from high blood pressure or heart problems, you should consult your doctor before engaging in this exercise.

## Visualisation

1. Choose a safe place to sit or lie down.

2. Imagine you are in a garden at the time of the year you like best, enjoying looking at flowers, shrubs, trees and so on.

3. You notice a wall along one side of the garden. In the middle of the wall is an old-fashioned wooden door with a wrought iron handle on it.

4. You make your way over to the door and open it.

5. On the other side, you find yourself in your own, very special, safe place. A place that no-one knows about and where no-one can get you.

6. Enjoy being there.

7. When you are ready, make your way back to the door.

8. Leave and shut the door firmly behind you, knowing that your special safe place is always there, whenever you choose to visit it.

9. Walk around the garden and, when you are ready, open your eyes.

**Note:** This exercise can take between two minutes and half an hour, depending on how much time you wish to allocate to it.

## Anchoring

'Anchoring' is a simple technique whereby you associate positive, calming, confident feelings to a particularly object, usually, (but not always) something you wear frequently. All that is required is that in moments of anxiety you touch the chosen object and then focus on the feelings associated with it.

1. Choose an object — say, a ring.

2. Now, close your eyes and focus on some aspect of your life that brings a warm glow or a smile to your face. This could be

a person, place, or an activity which makes you feel good about yourself.

3. Rub the ring as you reflect on that happy thought and continue doing so for five or more minutes.

4. Wait for a few minutes and then repeat the process.

5. In carrying out this simple routine, you will have anchored positive feelings to your chosen object. From now on, merely touching that object should bring on good feelings instantly.

## Anxiety and Dietary Tips

Anxiety can be made worse by taking stimulants such as tea, coffee, colas and chocolate, all of which contain caffeine. Caffeine is a stimulant which is best avoided when we are experiencing emotions such as anxiety and anger. Because we produce adrenaline when we are feeling anxious, this can affect our blood sugar levels, which may drop dramatically. Therefore, in order to keep those levels balanced, it is important to eat 'little and often' during the day. It may also be helpful to avoid refined sugars and other substances which 'give too much of a high' too quickly. Slow-release foods such as carbohydrates (potatoes, pasta, rice, bread, apples and bananas) are a much better idea, as they fuel the body in a more even, controlled way.

### Panic Attacks

Panic attacks are extremely common. Differences in the types of symptoms suffered are also extremely common. For example, one person may feel hot, another cold, so general guidelines apply.

### Panic Attack Checklist

If you are experiencing *4 or more of the following* symptoms you are probably experiencing panic attacks and would benefit from seeking professional help.

| *Symptom* | Yes | No |
|---|---|---|
| Palpitations, fast heart rate | | |
| Sweating | | |
| Shaking | | |
| Shortness of breath | | |
| A choking sensation | | |
| Chest pain | | |
| Nausea | | |
| Feeling dizzy | | |
| Feeling detached and unreal | | |
| Fear of dying | | |
| Tingling sensations | | |
| Chills and/or hot flushes | | |

**Note:** Although panic attacks are distressing, they are not usually life-threatening. However, as with any unusual physical symptoms, it is always safest to seek the advice of your doctor.

### Coping with Panic Attacks

- Remember that a panic attack is no more than an exaggeration of a normal bodily reaction to stress.

- Panic attacks are unpleasant, but will not harm you.

- Identify the self-defeating and frightening thoughts you engage in when you experience a panic attack, and counter these with the kind of thinking styles set out on pages 73–7 in the section on Negative Thinking. Adding to your self-defeating thinking will make matters worse, not better.
- Give the fear time to pass. Accept it, knowing that it will go away.
- Don't try and avoid your fear, as this will only make it worse. Facing your fear will help to diminish it, in time.
- When you feel better, plan what to do next.
- Think of the progress you are making every time you face your feelings, then praise yourself for facing your fear.

## Hyperventilation

Hyperventilation simply means 'over-breathing', something everyone does at some point. Sometimes, over-breathing is appropriate. Running for a bus, or some other kind of physical exertion requires more oxygen than normal, and so it's essential to breathe faster. However, if someone is not engaged in any kind of physical activity and is feeling anxious, they may begin to over-breathe, which can prove problematic. When too much oxygen enters the blood stream, it upsets the body's delicately balanced mechanism. The breathing exercise described above can help prevent you from hyperventilating. Remember to breathe in a controlled manner, as that is the key to combating this unpleasant feeling.

For some people, hyperventilation can bring on panic-attack-like symptoms. It is therefore crucial that you practice your breathing exercises on a daily basis. This use of controlled breathing (i.e. breathe in through the nose for a count of 4 and exhale through the mouth for a count of 5) will minimise the risk and effects of hyperventilation. Some people carry a paper bag with them and blow into this when they feel they are experiencing the effects of hyperventilation. This technique works because as we breathe out, we release carbon dioxide, so breathing this in again from the bag reduces the elevated levels of oxygen in the blood stream, thereby reducing the effects of the hyperventilation.

### Using Coping Imagery to Reduce Anxiety

We mentioned earlier that people who feel anxious often avoid situations. As a result, their lives may become very restricted. Often it requires much more than a simple decision to change that avoidance behaviour. Confronting a fear head on may prove to be too intimidating. For example, if you are claustrophobic and you haven't travelled on public transport for two years, then while using the rating scale outlined on page 167 (0 = no panic and 8 = major panic), you may experience a rating of 7 just thinking about the idea of boarding a train. Trying to force yourself to challenge that fear without making some kind of mental preparation could be enough to tip you over into a full-scale panic attack. A more effective tactic may be to use an imagery technique to prepare you for the event to help decrease your anxiety and practise the type of coping strategies that might be helpful. When anxiety levels have fallen to 4 or 5 using your rating, it may be the time to consider taking a real journey on public transport.

Coping imagery requires a person to imagine him or herself coping in a situation that usually causes them great fear. The following describes the sequence of action for dealing with a specific fear, say of travelling on a tube train.

### Maeve's Story

Maeve had seen a man jump in front of a underground train in London shortly after she had arrived from Ireland. She was just beginning to get to grips with the public transport system and was on her way to visit a historic site when the incident happened. Following this incident, she found it hard to travel on the underground and avoided doing so whenever she could. However, when she started a new job she realised the difficulty her avoidance behaviour was causing and decided to confront her fears. The following is based on the work that Maeve undertook to deal successfully with her problem.

1. First, write out a 'fears list', outlining a hierarchy of feared situations associated with underground travel using a scale of 0–8.

### Maeve's list

| | |
|---|---|
| Thinking about going to the local Underground station | = 3 |
| Getting my ticket | = 4 |
| Standing on the platform | = 5 |
| Getting onto a tube train | = 7 |
| Being stuck in a tunnel | = 8 |

2. Once you have this list made out, choose something from it that has a rating of no more than 4 or 5. (Choosing anything

with a higher rating would make it too difficult. A rating lower than 2 would probably not be challenging enough.)

Maeve decided to take standing on the platform, which she rated as a 5. She was then asked to imagine the following.

3. Now, close your eyes and imagine yourself standing on the platform.

Use all your senses to imagine the people on the platform, the sights and smells. Imagine yourself watching the trains come and go and monitor the anxiety you are feeling. Use coping strategies like breathing, anchoring and helpful self-talk to help yourself stay with the event. Maeve had already been taught how to relax through breathing. She had anchored a pleasant memory to a ring she always wore and she had been taught how her body worked, when anxious, in releasing adrenaline into the system and that her physical symptoms were normal. She had also put together some helpful self-talk, such as: 'This will pass. It is OK to be frightened, but nothing will happen to me, my anxiety will pass if I give it time.'

4. If you are using your coping strategies, your anxiety is likely to abate and once it has reduced to, say, a 3, you can choose something a little more difficult from the list you have drawn up.

Maeve practised this exercise for two days, three times a day until her anxiety had subsided to a 3. It was at this point that she decided to take a trip to her local underground station and undertake the exercise for real.

Maeve found that the exercise went well, and although her anxiety went up to a 5 when doing the exercise for real, it took very little time for it to subside. She used all her coping strategies and was very pleased with what she achieved. Her success gave her the confidence to increase the degree of difficulty using the items on her list. It took her just over ten days of regular daily practice to lose her fear of public transport.

To gain the maximum benefit from the above technique, you need to practise it frequently. Once you feel confident enough, you need to follow through with a real-life event. When you undertake a live exercise, you should use all the coping strategies you have practised in your imagination. It is also important to remember to break down your exercises into small manageable steps. Trying to do too much will put too much strain on you and could lead to a sense of failure. Remember that old maxim 'success breeds success'.

If you find it hard to use your imagination, try the following exercise to improve your visualisation skills and develop your imagination 'muscles'. Like everything else in life, with practice, your ability will improve:

- imagine looking at the sky at night
- choose one star and watch it become brighter and then dimmer. Do this repeatedly
- see if you can track the star across the sky.

CHAPTER 16

## *Life After Trauma*

The real troubles in life are apt to be things that never cross your mind until, suddenly, they blindside you one idle day when you are least expecting and least prepared for them. Traumatic events tend to fall into the category of life's uncontrollables. No-one is immune and someone has to be a statistic.

Trauma can be extremely painful psychologically, and while no therapist would recommend enduring trauma as some kind of character-building experience, for many people a personal trauma can prove to be the turning point that made their lives better in the long term. Even being a witness to a traumatic event can help reveal the importance of certain aspects of life — sometimes in ways not considered up to that point.

No sensitive person would ever say to someone in distress 'Look, in two or three years' time, you'll be a much better person for all this', but the fact is that many therapists' case files do contain 'happy outcome' footnotes. Many clients report back some years after trauma counselling with comments such as: 'Losing my job was the best thing that ever happened to me, because if I hadn't, I would never have become self-employed and I wouldn't be doing what I'm doing now.' Or: 'When I left my abusive partner with my two children and was forced to live in a refuge, it was a living hell. But if it hadn't have been for that I wouldn't now be happily settled with my children and have a loving new partner.'

Counsellors often say that working with trauma victims is one of the most fulfilling areas of their work. Trauma victims are normal people simply reacting to abnormal events. Anybody going through a trauma or trying to help someone they know through such a life crisis needs to look beyond what is happening and remind themselves that no-one remains in a state of crisis for ever. For some the crisis passes quickly and for others it takes longer. There is, of course, no time limit on how long or how sharply the memories of a trauma will linger. The important issue is how we use traumatic experiences to strengthen ourselves as individuals and how we use them to learn new coping skills.

As you will also know from reading the many case histories throughout this book, traumas such as a minor car accident, mugging or burglary often bring to the surface problems that have been niggling away for a long time, and which were not dealt with properly in the first place. A personal crisis may offer the opportunity to resolve problems previously unaddressed.

There is a very strong link between adversity and hope, in the sense that when we are facing adversity we hang on to the hope that something better is around the corner. By focusing on that hope, we somehow create our own luck and our own opportunity. The Chinese symbol for 'crisis' is a combination of two characters, one meaning 'danger' and the other 'opportunity'. I hope this book has helped to signpost some of the routes to finding the right kind of information and help to convert whatever life throws at you into an opportunity.

# Useful Addresses

## IRELAND

**AA Dublin Service Office**
109 South Circular Road, Leonards Corner, Dublin 8.
Tel. 01 453 8998.
*For those with an alcohol-related problem.*

**Aware — Helping to Defeat Depression**
147 Phibsborough Road, Dublin 7. Tel. 01 830 8449; helpline: 01 679 1711.
*Offers information, advice and counselling.*

**Bereavement Counselling Service**
Dublin Street, Baldoyle, Co. Dublin. Tel. 01 839 1766.
*Offers counselling and support.*

**Cluaiscint**
Tralee, Co. Kerry. Tel. 066 25932.
*Provides support for the families and friends of those bereaved by suicide.*

**Dublin County Stress Clinic**
St John of God Hospital, Stillorgan, Co. Dublin.
Tel. 01 288 1781.
*Specialist counselling services.*

## HEBER
c/o Irish Hospice Foundation, 9 Fitzwilliam Place, Dublin 2.
Tel. 01 676 5599.
*Umbrella organisation for hospice bereavement groups.*

## Irish Association for Counselling and Therapy
8 Cumberland Street, Dun Laoghaire, Co. Dublin.
Tel. 01 230 0061.
*Provides information, advice and details of counselling services.*

## Irish Council for Psychotherapy
17 Dame Court, Dublin 2. Tel. 01 679 4055.
*Offers information, advice and details of services.*

## Irish Friends of the Suicide Bereaved
PO Box 162, Cork. Tel. 021 294 318.
*Provides information, advice and counselling.*

## Rape Crisis Centre
70 Lower Leeson Street, Dublin 2. Tel. 01 661 4911; 1800 77 88 88.
*Offers information, advice, counselling and support.*

## Samaritans
112 Marlborough Street, Dublin 1. Tel. 01 872 7700; 1850 60 09 90.
*Telephone helpline for those who are suicidal and in crisis.*

## Solas — Bereavement Counselling for Children
Barnardo's, Christchurch Square, Dublin 8.
Tel. 01 453 0355.
*Offers information, advice and counselling.*

**Suicide Bereavement Support Group**
Tel. 01 848 4789.
*Offers counselling and support.*

**Victim Support**
29 Dame Street, Dublin 2. Tel. 01 679 8673.
*Offers information, advice, support and counselling to the victims of crime.*

# UNITED KINGDOM

**Alcohol Concern**
Waterbridge House, 32–36 Loman Street, London SE1 OEE.
Tel. 0207 928 7377.
*Provides information on alcohol and its effects. Can provide details of alcohol agencies, residential, advice and drop-in centres across the UK.*

**Association for Rational Emotive Behaviour Therapists**
St George's, Winter Street, Sheffield S3 7ND.
Tel. 0114 271 6926.
*Professional body for counsellors, psychologists and psychotherapists using REBT. Can provide details of such therapists.*

**BRAKE**
PO Box 272, Dorking, Surrey RH4 4FR.
Tel. 01306 741113.
*Provides information, advice and guidance for those involved in trauma following road traffic accidents.*

## British Association for Behavioural and Cognitive Psychotherapies

PO Box 9, Accrington BB5 2GD. Tel. 01254 875277.
*Professional body for psychiatrists, psychologists, counsellors and all those who use cognitive-behavioural techniques. Can provide lists of counsellors and also information on cognitive-behavioural psychotherapies.*

## British Association for Counselling

1 Regent Place, Rugby, Warwickshire CV21 2PJ.
Tel. 01788 578328.
*Professional body for counsellors in the UK. Can provide lists of counsellors and also information and advice on counselling.*

## British Psychological Society

St Andrew's House, 48 Princess Road East, Leicester LE1 7DR. Tel. 0116 254 9568.
*Professional body for psychologists. Can also provide details of psychologists.*

## Carers National Association

20 Glasshouse Yard, London EC1A 4JS.
Tel. 0207 490 8818.
*Association that provides help, advice and support to those who care for others.*

## Catalyst

Thames House, 65–67 Kingston Road, New Malden, Surrey KT3 3PB. Tel. 0208 949 7877.
*Help, information and advice for those dealing with young people.*

**Centre for Crisis Psychology**
Pinetum, Broughton Hall, Skipton, North Yorkshire BD23 3AE. Tel. 01756 796383.
*Specialist trauma counselling services.*

**Centre for Stress Management**
156 Westcombe Hill, Blackheath, London SE3 7DH.
Tel. 0208 293 4114.
*Provides information and advice on stress-related issues together with counselling and psychotherapy. Also offers training in a variety of subjects including stress and post-trauma stress to a range of professionals.*

**Changing Faces**
1–2 Junction Mews, London W2. Tel. 0207 706 4232.
*For those trying to come to terms with a changed physical appearance.*

**Child Bereavement Trust**
Tel. 01628 488101.
*Offers information, advice and support to anyone who has experienced the death of a child, and to bereaved children.*

**Child Traumatic Stress Clinic**
Department of Psychology, Institute of Psychiatry,
De Crespigny Park, Denmark Hill, London SE5 8AF.
Tel. 0207 919 3216.
*Offers counselling, advice and support to parents and to children who have experienced traumatic events.*

## Childline
Freepost 1111, London N1 OBR. Tel. 0800 1111.
*Offers information, advice, counselling and support to children experiencing any type of difficulty. Advice also available to parents.*

## Compassionate Friends
53 North Street, Bristol BS3 1EN. Tel. 0117 953 9639.
*Offers support to parents who have lost a child through illness, accident, murder or suicide.*

## COSCA (Confederation of Scottish Counselling Agencies)
64 Murray Place, Stirling FK8 2BX. Tel. 01786 475140.
*Professional body for counsellors in Scotland. Can provide details of counsellors and information on counselling and counselling services.*

## CRUSE Bereavement Care
Cruse House, 126 Sheen Road, Richmond, Surrey TW9 1UR. Tel. 0208 940 4818.
*Offers information, advice and counselling to those who have been bereaved. Local branch offices across the country.*

## Cult Information Centre
BCM, London EC1N 3XX. Tel. 0208 651 3322.
*Provides information, advice and counselling to those who have left or wish to leave a cult, as well as to families and friends of those in cults.*

## Depression Alliance
PO Box 1022, London SE1 7QB. Tel. 0207 633 9929.
*Information, advice and support for those who suffer from depression, including support for families and friends.*

**Divorce, Conciliation and Advisory Service**
38 Ebury Street, London SW1W OLU. Tel. 0207 730 2422.
*Provides information, advice, counselling and support.*

**Dover Counselling Centre**
9 Cambridge Terrace, Dover CT16 1YZ. Tel. 0304 204 123.
*Specialist counselling service.*

**Drinkline (The National Alcohol Helpline)**
Petersham House, 57 Hatton Garden, London EC1N 8HP.
Tel. 0345 320202.
*Offers advice, counselling and support to all those with alcohol-related problems.*

**EAC (European Association for Counselling)**
PO Box 82, Rugby, Warwickshire CV21 2AD.
Tel. 01788 546731.
*Provides details of counselling organisations in Europe.*

**Ex-Services Mental Welfare Society**
Broadway House, The Broadway, Wimbledon, London SW19 1RL. Tel. 0208 543 6333.
*Provides information, advice, counselling and support.*

**Families Need Fathers**
134 Curtain Road, London EC2A 3AR.
Tel. 0207 613 5060.
*Provides information, advice and support for parents experiencing difficulties with child access, or who are finding it difficult to come to terms with limited child access.*

**Inform (Information Network Focus On Religious Movements)**
Houghton Street, Aldwych, London WC2A 2AE.
Tel. 0207 955 7654.
*Provides information, advice and counselling for those concerned about the impact of religious institutions or cults on themselves or others.*

**International Stress Management Association (UK)**
Division of Psychology, South Bank University, 103 Borough Road, London SE1 OAA. Tel. 07000 780430.
*Provides information, advice and details of stress management practitioners and trainers.*

**Lifeline — Help for Victims of Violence in the Home**
6 Edward Street, Albert Village, Burton on Trent, Staffs DE11 8ER. Tel. 0332 774881.
*Provides information, advice and support.*

**Medical Foundation for the Care of Victims of Torture**
96 Grafton Road, London NW5 3EJ. Tel. 0207 284 4321.
*Offers help to anyone who has been the victim of torture.*

**National Council for One-Parent Families**
50 Lindley Street, London E1 3AX. Tel. 0207 267 1361.
*Offers information, advice and support on a range of issues affecting one-parent families.*

**Parent Network**
44–46 Caversham Road, London NW5 2DS.
Tel. 0207 485 8535.
*Provides information, advice and support to parents.*

## Parents Anonymous
6 Manor Gardens, London N7 6LA. Tel. 0207 263 8918.
*Offers information, advice, counselling and support to parents fearful of hurting their children.*

## Phobic Action
Greater London House, 547–551 High Road, London E11 4PB. Tel. 0208 558 6012 (helpline); 0208 558 3463 (office).
*Provides information, advice and counselling to those whose lives are affected by a phobia.*

## Post-Adoption Service
8 Torriano Mews, Torriano Avenue, London NW5 2RZ. Tel. 0207 284 0555.
*Offers helps in dealing with the issues raised by adoption, including locating birth parents and adopted children.*

## Rape Counselling Research Project
London Rape Crisis Centre, PO Box 69, London WC1X 9NJ. Tel. 0207 278 3956.
*Offers information, advice, counselling and support to male and female rape victims.*

## Relate
Herbert Gray College, Little Church Street, Rugby, Warwickshire CV21 3AP. Tel. 0870 601 2121.
*Provides counselling for couples.*

## Samaritans
10 The Grove, Slough, Berkshire. Tel. 01753 532713; 0345 90 90 90.
*Telephone counselling and drop-in centres.*

## USEFUL ADDRESSES

**Standing Conference on Drug Abuse**
1–4 Hatton Place, Hatton Garden, London EC1N 8ND.
Tel. 0207 430 2341.
*Provides information, advice and details of counselling for those affected by drug misuse.*

**Support after Murder and Manslaughter (SAMM)**
Cranmer House, 39 Brixton Road, London SW9 6DZ.
Tel. 0207 735 3838.
*Offers information, advice and support.*

**Survivors**
PO Box 2470, London SW9 9ZP. Tel. 0207 833 3737 (helpline).
*Support for men who have been raped.*

**Trauma Advisory Services**
c/o BRAKE, PO Box 272, Dorking, Surrey RH4 4FR.
Tel. 01306 741113.
*Offers specialist counselling for trauma victims.*

**Trauma Aftercare Trust (TACT)**
Buttfields, The Farthings, Withington, Gloucester GL54 4DF.
Tel. 01242 890306.
*Specialist trauma counselling services.*

**Traumatic Stress Clinic**
73 Charlotte Street, London W1P 1LB. Tel. 0207 436 9000.
*Specialist trauma counselling services — a national referral centre.*

**UKCP (United Kingdom Council for Psychotherapy)**
167 Great Portland Street, London W1N 5FB.
Tel. 0207 436 3002.
*Register of psychotherapists in the UK.*

**UKRC (United Kingdom Register of Counsellors)**
1 Regent Place, Rugby, Warwickshire CV21 2PJ.
Tel. 01788 550899.
*Register of counsellors in the UK.*

**Victim Support**
Cranmer House, 39 Brixton Road, London SW9 1DZ.
Tel. 0207 735 9166.
*Offers information, advice, counselling and support to those who have been the victims of crime. Local branches.*

**Women's Therapy Centre**
6–9 Manor Gardens, London N7 6LA. Tel. 0207 263 6200.
*Specialist counselling services.*

**Young Minds (Parents Information Service)**
102–108 Clerkenwell Road, London EC1M 5SA.
Tel. 0345 626376.
*Offers specialist counselling services for parents and their children.*

**Youth Access**
2 Taylor's Yard, Alderbrook Road, London SW12 8AD.
Tel. 0208 722 9900.
*Offers specialist youth counselling services.*

## WEB SITES

**American Family Foundation Cult Group Information**

http://www.csj.org/

**Cult Information Service**

http://www.member.aol.Com/shawdan/cis.htm

http://dir.yahoo.Com/Society and Culture/Religion/Cults

**Exclusive Brethren Information**

http://www.cloudnet.Com/~dwyman/pb.html

**Families Need Fathers**

http://www.fnf.org.uk

# Further Reading

Ainsworth-Smith, I. and Speck, P. *Letting Go: Caring for the Dying and Bereaved*, London: SPCK, 1999

Barbach, L. *For Each Other: Sharing Sexual Intimacy* London: Corgi, 1983

Barker, P. J. *A Self-Help Guide to Managing Depression* London: Stanley Thornes, 1993

Burns, D. *The Feeling Good Handbook* London: Plume, 1990

Childs-Gowell, E. *A Healing Companion: Good Grief Rituals, Tools for Healing* New York: Station Hill Press, 1992

Coleman, V. *Overcoming Stress* London: Sheldon Press, 1995

Dryden, W. *Overcoming Shame* London: Sheldon Press, 1997

Dryden, W. *Overcoming Guilt* London: Sheldon Press, 1994

Fennell, M. *Overcoming Low Self-Esteem: A Self-Help Guide using Cognitive-Behavioural Techniques* London: Robinson, 1999

Ghazi, P. and Jones, J. *Downshifting: The Guide to Happier, Simpler Living* London: Coronet Books, 1997

Hauck, P. *Calm Down: How to Cope with Frustration and Anger* London: Sheldon Press, 1980

Herbert, C. and Wetmore, A. *Overcoming Traumatic Stress: A Self-help Guide to using Cognitive-Behavioural Techniques* London: Robinson, 1999

Keane, C. *Nervous Breakdown* Cork: Mercier Press, 1994

Kennerley, H. *Overcoming Anxiety* London: Robinson, 1997

Lindenfield, G. *Managing Anger* London: Thorsons, 1993

Marks, I. *Living With Fear* London: McGraw Hill, 1980

Matsakis, A. *I Can't Get Over It: A Handbook for Trauma Survivors* California: New Harbinger Publications, 1992

O'Hanlon, B. *Sleep: The CommonSense Approach* Dublin: Gill & Macmillan, 1998

O'Hanlon, B. *Stress: The CommonSense Approach* Dublin: Gill & Macmillan, 1998

Palmer, S. and Burton, T. *People Problems at Work* London: McGraw Hill, 1996

Parkinson, F. *Post-trauma Stress* London: Sheldon Press, 1993

Quilliam, S. *Stop Arguing, Start Talking* London: Vermillion, 1998

Quilliam, S. *What To Do When You Really Want To Help But Don't Know How* London: Transformation Press, 1998

Rosenbloom, D. and Williams, M. B. *Life After Trauma* London: The Guildford Press, 1999

Sheridan, S. and Waugh, C. *Using Relaxation for Health and Success* London: How to Books, 1999

Silove, D. and Manicavasagar, V. *Overcoming Panic* London: Robinson, 1997

Stuart, W. *Building Self-Esteem: How to Replace Self-Doubt with Confidence and Well-Being* London: How to Books, 1998

Sweet, C. *Overcoming Addiction: Positive Steps for Breaking Free of Addiction and Building Self-Esteem* London: Piatkus Books, 1999

Tallis, F. *Understanding Obsessions and Compulsions: A Self-Help Manual* London: Sheldon Press, 1992

Tallis, F. *How to Stop Worrying* London: Sheldon Press, 1990

Tobias, M.L. and Lalich, J. *Captive Hearts, Captive Minds: Freedom and Recovery from Cults and Abusive Relationships* New York: Hunter House, 1994

Trickett, S. *Coping Successfully with Panic Attacks* London: Sheldon Press, 1992

Walther, A. M. *Divorce Hangover* London: Pocket Star Books, 1991

Van Der Zeil, E. *Perfect Relaxation* London: Arrow, 1996